# HOW THE RAILWAYS WILL FIX THE FUTURE

# HOW THE RAILWAYS WILL FIX THE FUTURE

Gareth Dennis

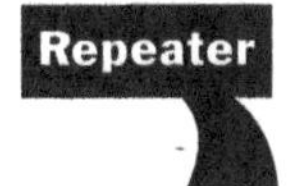

Published by Repeater Books

An imprint of Watkins Media Ltd

Unit 11 Shepperton House

89-93 Shepperton Road

London

N1 3DF

United Kingdom

www.repeaterbooks.com

A Repeater Books paperback original 2024

2

Distributed in the United States by Random House, Inc., New York.



ISBN: 9781915672483

Ebook ISBN: 9781915672506



Printed and bound by CPI Group (UK) Ltd, Croydon, CR0 4YY

Contents

# PREFACE

# TWO STRIPS OF STEEL

Like a missed train, the moment has passed. The point at which we could avoid a future that requires us to completely rethink how our society functions has come and gone.

We can no longer tinker around the edges of our society to keep it viable: humanity needs to embrace massive change — on a scale we've not yet truly conceived of. And this change will touch every aspect of the way we live our lives.

After food, shelter, safety and wellbeing, movement is one of humanity's basic needs. And the way we currently facilitate that movement has fuelled the biggest threat to our species.

Global warming, global heating, climate change: whatever you call it, it is the greatest existential crisis facing humanity. It is no longer possible to avoid its consequences — we can only do our best to minimise those consequences and their impact on society. Mitigation *of* and adaptation *to* the new climate: get this wrong and we deepen every other challenge we face, too.

This is not a future problem. Extreme weather events that test the resilience of our critical infrastructure have already increased in frequency thanks to climate change. It is happening now, and it is happening more. And the changes we are seeing now — and which we will see several decades into the future — are as a result of locked-in carbon emissions. The changes we make now are about how extreme climate change will be by the end of this century.

Consequently, we no longer have a choice about "if" — we only have a choice about "when", "how" and "for whom".

As Professor Kevin Anderson, jointly of the University of Manchester in the UK, Uppsala University in Sweden and Bergen University in Norway, says:

> There are now no non-radical futures. The choice is between immediate and profound social change, or waiting a little longer for chaotic and violent social change. In 2023, the window for this choice is rapidly closing.[1]

As I write this, it is 2024, and globally, transport now accounts for a third of end-use emissions and a fifth of total emissions from all sources. On a planet-wide basis, it is the second-largest sectoral contributor to emissions after energy and heat production.

In most developed economies, transport is *the largest* sectoral source of greenhouse gas emissions. In other words, as both energy efficiency and the decarbonisation of electricity generation have borne fruit, transport now accounts for more emissions than any other sector. As the number of developed economies increases, so too will the number of countries where transport accounts for the biggest portion of their emissions.

If transport is the largest source of carbon emissions for a given country, then road transport will always account for the vast majority of those emissions. In the UK, road

---

[1] Mike Small (2023) "There Are No Non-Radical Futures", *Bella Caledonia*, 18 April, available online at: https://bellacaledonia.org.uk/2023/04/18/no-radical-futures/

transport alone accounts for 25% of our total emissions (rail accounts for 0.4%). Most of this comes from long-distance journeys, not short trips, so shifts to active travel (walking, cycling, etc.) can only achieve so much.

Right now, this leaves most governments and many environmentalists under the impression that a straight conversion from combustion engines to battery motors will solve the emissions crisis and save the future. They could not be more wrong. Electric car take-up is too slow to make a tangible difference to greenhouse gas emissions compared to the rapidly increasing quantity of private cars still burning fossil fuels. Heavier battery-laden cars put more strain on road surfaces and structures and increase fatalities from crashes. Road vehicles already account for the majority of plastic particulates in our air and oceans. More still, they require significant energy to manufacture, which remains hugely resource intensive as carmakers push ever larger vehicles onto consumers.

Critical, though, is that retaining the status quo of private, individualised transport locks in all of the existing inequalities of transport that we have today and does nothing to widen access to mobility for all of society. Reliance on electric road vehicles reinforces all of the existing power structures — benefiting automotive manufacturers, finance companies, resource extractors, housing developers and the rest — that have led us to this point in the first place and which have maintained the barriers between the global north and south, between rich and poor, in place.

Brazilian trade unionist, social activist and environmentalist Chico Mendes famously said: "Environmentalism without class struggle is just gardening."

Mendes was murdered by the son of a logging rancher for successfully standing up against the rancher's forced deforestation of falsely acquired land. His words resonate today and should act as an eternal check on the aims of today's campaigners for climate action — particularly people like me: white males with above-average incomes. What are the ramifications of what I'm proposing for people less well off than me? For women? For people of colour? For indigenous populations?

What other option is there? Any degrowth agenda that would essentially freeze carbon emissions per country as they are now would be a grossly discriminatory act, perpetuating the status quo benefiting consumers broadly in the global north. Humanity can do better than that. We have the ingenuity and the resources to enable shared prosperity and equality without restricting the poorest in society. As Professor Anderson says, we can either choose to be radical and control our collective destinies, or we can wait for a radical future to be inflicted upon us by the planet on which we reside.

This is where railways come in.

Two strips of steel rail are capable of carrying tens of millions of tonnes of traffic a year, potentially tens of thousands of people an hour, reaching speeds as high as 600 km/h, and they are replicated for hundreds of thousands of kilometres across the planet. Those rails, rolled to micron accuracies and ultrasound scanned to ensure flawlessness to the microscopic scale, are held apart at a distance defined by a chippy Geordie two centuries ago. The trains, each many tens, hundreds or thousands of tonnes in size, run on contact patches the size of your thumbnail, creating pressures intense enough to liquify steel.

Railways are both the past and future of human mobility. They are the safest and most energy-efficient means of mass transport we've conceived of and likely ever will conceive of. Star Trek transporter technology may materialise at some point, but not until we've unlocked one or more sources of limitless energy, and not before the climate ravages our society and changes our priorities drastically.

Until that point, trains are the future. And in this book I intend to explain why it is so crucial that we fix what's wrong with them so that they can unleash their full potential against humanity's greatest threats. Because global warming is upon us, and there's no running from it. The changing climate is intensifying extreme weather and battering infrastructure and supply chains both locally and globally. Responding to the need for greater robustness and resilience in the face of this onslaught requires a greater number of engineers and skilled people, and making the best use of them means relying on systems that move more people with less infrastructure. That means mass transit, not roads.

Climate change and current patterns of human development are exacerbating and accelerating biosphere fragmentation and collapse. Rail has a vital role to play in minimising urban sprawl, reducing land take and stitching once-fragmented habitats back together.

Consumerism, the rampant capitalism it fuels and the consequent unchecked race for resources result in the mass exploitation of labour in the global south, including children, who are already the most vulnerable to the effects of climate change. By reducing consumerism and alleviating the mineral-hungry forms of energy consumption associated with the car-dominated societies we currently live in, railways can end this exploitation.

Modern supply chains — not least those for food — have been exposed as highly vulnerable. There is plenty of food in the world to ensure everybody is well fed if only we could distribute it more fairly among ourselves. There are clearly bigger factors at play, but the cost savings that improved transportation will represent must be reflected in increased wages and reduced prices and not be seen as an opportunity to increase profit margins further.

Further, the erosion of democracy and rise of populism have been facilitated by false scares around migration, when in most cases it is the erosion of local democracy and public services — as well as the effects of globalisation and redistribution of jobs — that has impacted communities. By facilitating the flow of people around the globe and raising living standards in areas currently exploited for cheap labour, these effects can be mitigated by an enhanced global railway system.

Instead, widening transport poverty and inequality — in many cases worsened by the permanent reduction of public transport services following the COVID-19 pandemic — now present another facet of the problem. The cost of moving around is a burden for those trying to access employment, education and — even today — clean water and food. Access to public services, too, is limited by car dominance and dependence. It is imperative, therefore, that safe, accessible and frequent public transport options are available for everyone, globally.

Automation, isolation, disinformation, radicalisation and war: these are not discrete challenges; they are all interlinked, with each having an impact on all the rest. Usefully, this means that a single tool, chosen and applied correctly, can have meaningful, lasting and significant positive impacts on all of these challenges at once. Thus, rail isn't just one tool in a toolbox to resolve these challenges — it can be the key to tackling many of them. Only rail provides the balance of capability and efficiency that can respond to the needs of our future society, fostering the necessary skills, spaces and structures that it takes for us to thrive in spite of the challenges we've created for ourselves.

Further, the lessons to be learned from creating, operating and maintaining railways can be directly applied to other domains, giving us insights that can provide solutions well outside the domain of transport and spatial planning.

In short, radically improving human transit is one of the most important projects for our species over the next half century.

This picture of complex, multifaceted and interlinked challenges, threatening as it may be, has its equal in the might and power of what humanity can offer in its collective tenacity and ingenuity. Indeed, humanity has all the skills and tools to tackle this burgeoning omnithreat today, and knowing this gives me great optimism for the future if we can only tap into this capability.

Across the world we can see how the collective efforts of humanity, driven by the right incentives, can not only overcome adversity on any scale, but can do so fairly and quickly. Shared knowledge and understanding of the physical and social sciences has prepared us to make the most of the skills and resources we have access to. Engineering harnesses these sciences, and with a tested ethical framework it can be the engine that unleashes our collective energy, skills and knowledge to overcome the enormous shared adversity of this century. I may be a cynic, but thinking about this gets me excited almost beyond words.

There's a problem, though.

If the world is in crisis, most railways across the world are in crisis, too, and at a time when they are most needed.

The crippling of the British rail industry shows no sign of abating, despite passengers gritting their teeth and returning to rail in their droves. Indeed, as the flailing UK government has tightened its control over the industry, increasingly disruptive waves of industrial action have brought the system to a near-total standstill on multiple occasions.

Across the Atlantic, the entire US railroad system was on the brink of grinding to a halt in 2022, with waves of national strikes scheduled for December. At the eleventh hour, legislation signed by President Biden forced unions to accept an unfavourable deal in order to prevent chaos. The purpose of these strikes? To save an industry intent on grinding itself out of existence as its enormous private owners chased their manufactured god known as the "operating ratio". With the strikes called off, the problem has merely been kicked a year or two down the road. Great work, Amtrak Joe.

Hopping back over to Europe, and to a country often (falsely) associated with reliable railways, Germany had its rail network shut down in March and April 2023 as striking workers walked out. Prior to the strikes, 2022 saw Germany only running two-thirds of its trains on time. Things have only gotten worse since.

In the aftermath of COVID-19, and with an ever-ageing population, Japan's railways faced the shutdown not just of rural lines but of some of its main line services as persistent low uptake tipped the balance of subsidy in a direction the central government did not like, and the perception of rail as an unalloyed good was shaken.

But what is going on? If railways are so good, why are railway systems in these massive economies failing their workers and their passengers? What are they getting wrong? And what of the railway systems that work well? Where are they? What can we learn from them?

This book is split into three parts: in the first, we'll answer all of these questions by looking at the choices facing us when it comes to the future of human mobility. Exploring what railways are and where they came from will help us to understand why they aren't a transient or superseded technology. We'll then dig into the mechanics and politics of why railways aren't reaching their full potential today, taking a global tour of railway systems to see where rail is succeeding, and where it is not.

To really prove why rail is (or at least has the potential to be) supreme, you have to look at the alternatives, be they road, air or vapourware nonsense. Doing so also lets us see the forces of capital that are being leveraged against rail and society at large, and why rail must thrive to overcome them.

In the second part, we'll set out a ten-point manifesto for fixing the railways and harnessing them to build a fairer future — to shape today's into tomorrow's railways. I'll explain how to develop a plan from the right incentives, and how to shape the railways and wider democratic structures to deliver it while maximising public accountability.

No plan can be delivered without skilled people, so we'll also look at growing the right workforce, the barriers preventing this from happening and why empowering and organising labour is the only way to achieve it.

When thinking about rail workers, it is impossible to ignore the influence of technology and automation in particular, so understanding the relationship between railways and tech is crucial. In turn, we can see how technology will shape how railways survive the challenges of the future, not only that of changing climate, but also the threat of cyber-attacks and the dominance of big corporations.

With all of this under our belt, we must answer the most important question of all: Who should the railways be for? Today's railways exclude too many, either through a lack of accessibility or through high fares — this must stop. But the work cannot end there — indeed, how we tell the story of the railways' role in society is as important as getting the railways themselves right.

In the third part of the book, we'll step back and paint a vibrant picture of what the optimal railway system must look like, and present a timeline for the actions we need to get there. You cannot build the future if you cannot imagine it.

Throughout the book, my hope is not just to describe how railways fit into the future, but also how they can act as a lens through which to filter and understand what future we want to see, allowing us to think clearly about our relationship with organised labour, with technology and with democratic principles.

Given recent industrial action regarding rail in the UK and US, rail travel's surge in popularity across mainland Europe and rail construction being used as a tool of Chinese imperialism in sub-Saharan Africa, the railways are becoming politically relevant in a way they haven't been since the nineteenth century. The trouble is that they remain a mystery to many, and over-simplified rhetoric is often accompanied by bad policy choices or poor campaigning from otherwise progressively minded people. The grim reality is that the left has fallen out of love with railways — or perhaps it never fell in love with them in the first place.

My hope is that this book will reunite those with a hopeful, equitable and progressive view of the future — those on the left — with the power of the railways and act as a handbook to cut through the complexity of railway policymaking, painting an international picture of how the railways can not only play a role in creating a brighter future, but actually provide a template for that future.

This isn't a technical book; I've written it for everyone. But neither is it *not* a technical book. There ought to be something in it for everyone.

My hope, should you reach the end of it, is that you'll not only be excited about a future society in which safe, democratised and accessible railways are its circulatory system, but that your imagination of the possibilities for the future will be sufficiently fizzing that you'll be explaining why to anyone who'll listen.

It isn't because I'm a railway engineer that I see railways as the conduit through which we can channel this opportunity, but hopefully, as a railway engineer, I can explain how.

# PART 1

# THE CHOICE

# CHAPTER 1.1

# WHY MOBILITY MUST CHANGE

Humanity is ailing.

In the consuming countries, generally those in the global north, increased individualism is leading us into greater populism, paranoia and selfishness. The way we move around is only exacerbating this — driving has been shown to make us more aggressive, violent and self-centred. The academics call it "motonormativity", the rest of us call it "car brain".

In the countries that create rather than consume, the individualism of the global north has led to economic dependence, exploitation of labour, environmental ruin and greater exposure to the consequences of climate change.

Nevertheless, as the favoured economic system of the global north continues to decay, growing less and less capable of responding to the needs of the people relying on it, those countries considered "developing" continue to build power on the global stage. This isn't limited to China and India, either. Nigeria, for example, flexes its economic and cultural prowess and consequently acts as a political pivot point for Russia, China, Europe and the US in West Africa.

The complacency of liberal politics, deluded with the belief that democracy is self-sustaining and can withstand deepening inequity, means that many countries in the global north have slid further back into populism and authoritarianism. The massive centralisation of power with a very small number of billionaires and corporations, combined with the trend towards disempowering local in favour of national (and indeed pan-national) governments, has exacerbated the feelings of isolation, powerlessness and indifference already forged by our current economic system and its manifestations in the built environment.

Those in power are therefore desperate for patterns of mobility to stay the same. For them, mobility within cities and countries must favour those who can afford to drive or fly. They see international mobility as a tool to bolster capital, not to bring us closer together. The movement of people across borders can only be permeable where it facilitates economic growth rather than, say, providing safe haven for those displaced by extreme weather or violence, or even for those who wish to build a new life in another part of the world. Change represents a risk to the established order of things — a threat that wealth might no longer be extracted as egregiously as it currently is.

This presents us with a choice. We can stick with current forms of mass mobility, which the world over are based around individualised transport — both for people and to a significant extent for goods — using roads, physically and socially segregating our society, widening and entrenching existing inequalities, de-socialising the built environment, shattering communities and turbo-charging consumerism, handing our future to those who have already done their best to destroy it.

Alternatively, as the tech industry would have us and our governments believe, we can wait around for fantasy solutions that, with only a little prodding, are soon revealed to be barely different from today's dominant mode: the car.

Or we can choose to take the system that we know is the safest, fastest and most efficient, the system that allows us to take our public spaces back, that gives us our time back, that gives us our breathable air back, and we can deploy it at a scale that renders the alternatives significantly obsolete. If our society is to tackle its biggest challenges, then the railways are surely one of the most powerful tools we have to instigate that change.

Social mobility requires actual mobility, and building better public transport systems with rail as their backbone can help reverse the localised effects of an economic system that's decidedly anti-local. In the global north, car ownership reduces relative to household income; for example, in the UK, fewer than half of households in the bottom fifth of income have access to a car. In the global south, this is only exaggerated. Reversing car dependence is a critical step in reducing poverty and social inequality.

Better public transport can enable a far more widespread proliferation of other public services by centralising their delivery without locking people into having to use cars to access them. On the flip side, building a society that relies on people having to own, maintain, insure, operate and drive cars to access services, employment, leisure and care results in a greatly widened economic divide between those who have time and money to drive and those who do not.

If you build an economic system (and the physical environment that enables it) specifically to isolate people by design, then of course you will be creating unsustainable levels of isolation for those living in that system, not just of older people but for anyone disadvantaged, disabled, dispossessed or otherwise dissociated from their fellow humans by the world around them. Many people currently suffering alone or dependent on support would otherwise be enjoying mostly autonomous lives if we hadn't created cities that were hostile to human needs in favour of the needs of metal boxes on wheels.

One billion people on this planet are disabled by their surroundings, with the system set up to ensure that they have trouble accessing healthcare, employment and education. Consequently, they are more likely to live below the poverty line. Reversing this situation requires more than just a reversal of car dominance. Public transport is still built to be inaccessible for many disabled people, and action to improve access is often disjointed or prevents truly independent and anxiety-free travel. Rail is guilty of this in many cases, but its inherent design also means it is very well suited to provide freedom of travel for disabled people.

With the choice of what future mobility will look like before us, railways ought to be the obvious answer. But they are not perfect — indeed, while the car has accelerated the decay of our species since the middle of the last century, it was the railways that created the structures of wealth distribution that entrenched power in the global north. Today, they are still harnessed as a weapon by those who have power against those who do not.

Any change in mobility must be accompanied by a change in the distribution of power, lest we continue to embed the problems we are trying to solve.

In other words, we need to understand and acknowledge the darker corners of railway history to avoid repeating the same evils.

However, railways across the globe are already providing us better alternatives. As our populations urbanise, the world's already-thriving megacities rely on a pulsating circulatory system of urban transit, moving hundreds of millions of people a day safely and cleanly. Where railways are prioritised as part of a wider, integrated public transport system, people are happier, healthier and freer to enjoy time with friends and family, engage with their culture and generally do the things that enrich our lives.

It's about time we collectively made our mobility choice.

# CHAPTER 1.2

# THE RAILWAYS: WEAPON OR TOOL?

No discussion of railways and their role in society can really start without understanding what they fundamentally are, how they work, what the physical — but also metaphorical — moving parts look like and how they were developed.

Furthermore, historical context is critical, and ignoring the dark past of railways prevents us from harnessing them for good in the future. Resource extraction, war, slavery and genocide have all been enabled by railways. Why is this? How do we tackle this legacy, and how do we prevent it in the future?

With their benefits having traditionally favoured the powers of empire and capital that wielded them, the railways have — uncomfortably for their proponents — repeatedly been a force for ill throughout modern history. However, they have achieved this by relying on fundamentals that have been and can continue to be harnessed for enormous good.

Understanding these fundamentals informs us how to best apply the power of the railways to the challenges we face and provides us with a toolkit to understand why their alternatives, real or fictional, fall short.

## What is a railway?

Firstly, what are the Railways (as opposed to railways)? Well, as I see it, railways are just the physical stuff, tracks, trains and so on. The Railways take those bits and pieces and combine them with the people who run the thing, the skills and pathways required to keep that pool of people topped up, and the democratic mandate and leadership required to keep pushing the whole thing forwards.

The distinction is important because policymakers and indeed engineers can often think of the railway as merely the sum of its physical bits, but this forgets that the whole thing falls apart without skilled practitioners holding it together and keeping it moving, let alone specifying and building it in the first place.

I'm going to drop the capitalisation as there's nothing worse than a writer inventing jargon. When I talk about the railway, you'll know what I mean.

But what, materially, is a railway?

A railway is, at its most fundamental, a transport system relying on two rails set a fixed distance apart that provide support and guidance to the vehicles travelling on it.

Two features set this arrangement apart from surfaced roads — that the interface between the wheel and rail is designed to minimise rather than maximise friction, and that the vehicle is guided by the rails, rather than guiding itself. Both features are critical to the success of the railways, and for better and for worse enabled railways to deliver us the modern world as we know it.

But what came first?

## The history nobody tells you about

Contrary to popular belief, the Romans were not the first to build decent roads. Long-distance tracks, ridgeways and other engineered paths have been in use since Neolithic times.

In the USA, indigenous populations followed, laid and reinforced paths across their lands for communication and trade, in many cases taking advantage of the routes worn into the earth by migratory bison and other animals. In the case of Algonquian- and Iroquoian-speaking peoples, their complex network of paths became known collectively as the Great Path, with much of this extensive infrastructure forming the basis of the modern US road system in the northeast.

While the precise age of these networks of pathways is not known, they are considered some of the most ancient lines of communication on our planet.

The oldest known constructed trackways in the world can be found in the UK, dating back nearly six thousand years and built with prepared strips of timber to enable passage through the marshlands of the Somerset Levels. The oldest paved road is located in Egypt and is slightly less ancient, being around 4,400 years old. And while they weren't the first to build paved roads, the Romans were certainly the most prolific, building tens of thousands of stone-paved roads across their empire up to its peak around 1,900 years ago.

These ancient paths, tracks and roads provided a firm, drained surface for people to use, mostly on foot, and latterly for livestock and horses. But they were not designed specifically to reduce friction for and guide vehicle wheels.

The first example of a system that exhibits the fundamentals of a railway is not nearly as notable as the immense network of roads built by the Romans, but it certainly precedes it. In southern central Greece, and operating as long as 2,600 years ago, the Diolkos provided a paved trackway, but with grooves cut into it a set spacing apart to enable wheeled carriages with small ships resting on top to be hauled between the Ionian and Aegean seas — incidentally, at around 1,600 mm, this was not dissimilar to modern track gauge at 1,435 mm. The track was built in hard limestone to minimise friction and was successful enough to establish a reputation across ancient Greece as a uniquely speedy form of transportation. It can even be argued that, given the Diolkos was recorded as being open to any fee-paying users, this was the first public railway. Operating for at least six centuries, it would be nearly two millennia before the concept of the public railway would be revisited.

However, the use of a *permanent way* (as a trackway that uses two grooves or rails fixed a set distance apart can be usefully named) would emerge into common use more recently. The first recorded description of the use of a permanent way system after Diolkos was in Austria, with a funicular (cable on a steep slope) track relying on two wooden "rails" carrying vehicles hauled by rope up to the Hohensalzburg Fortress. The *Reisszug* is still operating today — albeit with somewhat updated technology — but its operation was first written about in 1515 and potentially dates back to 1495.

The use of these systems became widespread across the German-speaking world, and by 1556 the first contemporary illustration of a "train" was made by Georgius Agricola, showing mine carts on wooden wheels traversing wooden planks and using a pin for guidance.

German practitioners of mine engineering (engineers still hadn't been invented yet) brought their contraptions to the UK within a decade, and built the first wagonways in rain-swept Cumbria. By the end of that century, wagonways were popping up across Central Europe and England.

It took another century and a half before wagonways found their way across the Atlantic, with the first one operating in the United States in Lewiston, New York, in 1764.

The technology of wagonways was now moving on at pace. Thanks to a reasonably unique combination of purity and accessibility, "coking" coal mined in the little village of Coalbrookdale in Shropshire enabled the smelting of a more cheaply produced and superior-quality iron, and it quickly found use formed into plates and laid on top of the wooden wagonway rails located nearby.

From this point, the development of the permanent way was focused primarily in the UK. Within a couple of decades, the iron plates were being formed into an L-shape on which wheels would ride, or into what was called an "edge rail", relying on a smaller contact point between a flanged wheel and a narrower iron rail. In 1796, the first railway available for public use using edge rails was opened as the *Lake Lock Rail Road Company* in West Yorkshire. By the twilight of the eighteenth century, cast-iron rails were being used internationally as far afield as the United States and Russia, but these were all exported from the UK. However, cast iron was a poor material for the increasing loads they were carrying, and it took stocky northern metallurgist Henry Cort to improve on several existing techniques to "puddle" and roll wrought iron into more durable and longer iron rails. This also resulted in rails that were significantly cheaper to produce.

Wagonways, plateways and the new railways all relied on a mixture of rope, gravity and animal haulage. The Cornish engineer Richard Trevithick decided to harness the steam engine — now a well-established technology as the industrial revolution gained momentum — for a "self-motive" vehicle that could haul a train of wagons on these rails. His novel use of high-pressure steam enabled a relatively small but powerful machine.

On 21 February 1804, one of his steam locomotives hauled a line of wagons along the Penydarren tramway in South Wales. However, with cast-iron rails still being extensively used, Trevithick's locomotives proved too heavy for widespread application.

It took George Stephenson, the plucky Northumbrian engineer (engineers had finally been invented), to arrange all the pieces into a coherent system, and it wasn't until 1830 with the opening of the Liverpool and Manchester Railway that George, along with his son Robert, introduced the world to the first modern railway system.

Stephenson's masterpiece unified each of the fundamental elements of the modern railway that had been developed over the preceding century or two: timetables, signalling, double track and exclusive use by locomotive-hauled trains. However, the subsequent explosion in railway development was not simply a consequence of the technological pieces falling into place. At the same time, the transatlantic slave trade was being wound down in Britain. Directed towards an already proven and now refined technology was an entire industry of business interests, personnel, expertise and — to a smaller but no less significant extent — capital from slave-won activities or post-abolition slave-owner compensation. When redirected into the railways, their expansion accelerated unstoppably.

The Liverpool and Manchester Railway was very much conceived to carry slave-won goods from the docks of Liverpool to the cotton mills of Manchester and its surrounding conurbation. Across Britain, many new railways were built to move materials won by slavery, indentured servitude or an exploited domestic working class to fire the engines and forge the tools of empire. Directors, managers, clerks and political interests were redirected towards this new means of capital extraction.

At the other end of the supply chain, materials were obtained by and entirely without benefit to indigenous populations using railways as fractal arteries, pulling resources to the coasts for shipment.

Those in Britain didn't have to travel far to see a network built purely for resource extraction — the lines snaking up into the South Wales valleys like so many tendrils are a classic example of lines built to extract mineral wealth for a colonial power. Cuba and Jamaica saw some of the first railways built outside of the UK and US, specifically to extract sugar from slave plantations. This pattern was repeated over and over again across the globe, including on the African continent following the period of "New Imperialism" from the middle of the 1800s to the early 1900s.

Often cited by apologists for empire as a force for good, India's railways were envisaged as a racket for the East India Company to convert Indian taxes into shareholder income — and British protectionism ensued when it came to staffing and equipping the railway, further locking out local workers and communities well into the middle of the twentieth century. Of course, these railways were used to extract mineral wealth, but they also played a key role in the military subjugation of India's population.

The railways' use in the deployment of military force started soon after the steam locomotive proved capable of outpacing the speed of a horse. Trains first transported the Third Battalion Grenadier Guards alongside a contingent of the Royal Horse Artillery from London to Manchester, helping to break the 1842 general strike and allowing heavy repercussions against the first national mass movement driven by the working classes.

That same decade (and resulting from similar working-class tendencies then sweeping Europe), the Kingdom of Prussia used railways to deploy three battalions to defeat revolutionaries in Dresden, and railways enabled the Russian Empire to rescue the Austrian Empire from defeat in Hungary against similar opponents.

If a railway built by imperial or colonial forces wasn't primarily engaged in the extraction of resources or manufactured goods from an exploited land or population, then it is highly likely it was built to move military forces to enable expansion or subjugation.

More recently, the railways enabled warfare on a previously impossible scale in two world wars, and in the second of these permitted the mass deportation and genocide of — among others — millions of Jewish and Roma people across mainland Europe.

We'll talk about the frontiers of capitalism in later chapters, but the technological success of the modern railway system unlocked capitalism's greatest frontier by creating a planet-wide system of lines of communication.

## Fundamental principles

I've taken us on this brief historical detour mostly to make the point that the railways are not a recent, transient invention. They are as ancient and steadfast a means of moving people and things around as roads are.

However, it is impossible to consider the railways as separate from their legacy and the politics which created, sustained and in many cases now constrains them. They undoubtedly have a long history of being used to exploit people, both those whose land the railways barrelled through, and also the workers who operated (and continue to operate) them. Given all this, should they still form a part — indeed a critical component — of a sustainable future for humankind?

Those fundamental principles which enabled them to dominate transport until the middle of the twentieth century still apply — the laws of physics work the same today as they did in ancient Greece.

Thanks to the very low friction between the steel wheel and steel rail, railways can move a load using as little as 15% of the energy that road haulage needs. Across the European Union, the greenhouse gas emissions of a train journey (per passenger mile) are a quarter of those of a car journey, and a fifth of those of taking a plane.

How exactly does this work?

The railway owes its endurance to the fact that the engineering principles of the system permit a high level of control over the distribution of loads. Stress is transferred from the wheel onto the rail, through the track system, and down into the formation and supporting structures. This is known as the principle of load transfer, and the ability to control each of these interfaces allows engineers to design a system that is unbeatably energy efficient.

The most important of these interfaces is between the wheel and the rail. The strength of steel means there need only be a very small contact patch between the wheel and the rail, no larger than a thumbnail. Such a small area means friction is kept very low. The pneumatic tyre requires a contact patch — and therefore friction value — that is much larger. Greater friction means more energy is required to move a given load.

For every 100 miles a train hauls one tonne, a road vehicle can only haul it 35 miles using the same amount of energy. This translates to a colossal advantage in terms of pulling power: one locomotive can haul the equivalent of up to eighty heavy goods vehicles.

## The ultimate open-source tech

The track gauge is the distance between the inside faces of the two running rails. Breaks in track gauge make running trains on multiple companies' lines expensive and inefficient. As a result, in the UK, the Royal Commission for Railway Gauges was tasked with setting a standard track gauge to allow a freer flow of goods and passengers. The standard track gauge in Britain and across much of the globe — approximately 55% of the world's railways use it — is set to 1,435 mm. It is one of the fundamental dimensions that makes the railways work, and standardising this dimension might be the most important decision made in the history of open-source technology. For better or worse, it gave us the modern industrial age.

While many of its constituent components and subsystems may well be individually proprietary, the overall railway system was possibly the first industrial-scale example of open-source technology. The German miners who shared their original track design did so without limitation on its subsequent use, and the Stephensons shared their designs for the modern railway system keenly with friends and fellow engineers both across Britain and beyond. Nowadays, huge rafts of publicly accessible standards define interoperable railway systems that any competent designer and contractor can deploy.

As a result, the skills associated with railways can be readily recorded, shared and passed on, independent of organisational boundaries or international borders. And as much as possible, the international railway community likes to copy with pride.

This skill-sharing has been going on since the dawn of the railways back in the days of wooden mining tracks, but facilitated by the communication age, academia and the rise of professional institutions, has greatly expanded the links between nations and domains, allowing a free flow of knowledge and experience which has only improved railways and increased their benefits for society.

Appearing in front of the Royal Commission for Railway Gauges in 1845, Robert Stephenson made the following statement: “If I had been called upon to do so, it would be difficult to give a good reason for the adoption of an odd measure — 4 feet 8 and a half inches.” Yet the widespread adoption of this measure, largely independent of borders or national politics, changed the world, and it can change it again.

# CHAPTER 1.3

# WHERE RAILWAYS WORK (OR DON'T)

In reclaiming railways as the key tool for unlocking greater collective freedom and prosperity, we thankfully do not have to make a standing start. Even in the countries where the railways are a complete shambles (yep, I'm talking about the UK; we'll get there), they still shift enormous numbers of people and goods and have expansive and advanced systems in place to facilitate this while maximising safety.

The railway networks that really thrive, though, are the ones that are seen by their controlling powers as facilitating greater mobility (rather than as profit-generating ventures that happen to move people or goods around).

Every railway system is a product of its history and the culture within which it was and continues to be developed. This is true at city, regional and national levels. To develop a railway system fit for the future, a country's railway needs the following: (1) an empowered and integrated industry structure; (2) one that is aligned with and accountable to national, regional and city governments; (3) staff who are valued and comfortable; (4) high levels of investment; (5) a long-term plan; (6) a policy framework that looks at all transport as a whole.

If we are to understand how the railways are a key component in delivering us a better future, we need to know where they are already working very well. It's no good tearing things down and starting again — much of the world's railways are already delivering that better future today.

Comparing various national systems across the world allows us to learn what works and doesn't work, and to explore the enormous variations that constitute different systems' advantages.

To do this, I undertook a lengthy trawl through as much consistent and comparable railway data as I could find. Doing so has allowed me to create a Top Twenty list of national railway systems based on their raw effectiveness at carrying people and goods versus other modes of transport. These countries fall into some useful categories: those that are "underperforming with style", those "delivering", two "grossly imbalanced" systems and the "elites".

We'll list the Top Twenty off later — first we need to dig into the successes and failures of these networks and consider what we must learn from them to enable mobility that is optimised for the people and industries using them.

As I see it, there are four factors worth digging into in more detail which are largely responsible for today's flawed railway operations, and the biggest of them all comes down to a classic mistake in the reading of statistics.

## 1. Liberalisation has chased, not created, demand

The liberalisation and privatisation of railway systems in Europe is regularly claimed by politicians and liberal commentators to be the cause of the increase in patronage seen since the turn of the millennium. However, this conflates correlation and causation, and is usually the consequence of people looking at graphs with deceptive x-axes.

In 1990, things were looking up for Britain's railways: ridership had been climbing solidly since the mid-1980s; the average subsidy was as low as 20% of running costs, making the British system one of the most efficient in Europe; Thameslink was providing the first high-capacity suburban rail link through London, with Crossrail planning well advanced; the Transpennine Route Upgrade was being developed, intended to deliver electric services between Manchester and Leeds; and British Rail was planning for new high-speed rail links between the Channel Tunnel, London and the North of England.

Then the early-1990s recession hit. More than a decade of constrained public spending and service sell-offs meant that there was an immediate impact on passenger numbers, which sent government into a panic. Suddenly, the doctrine of "sell everything but the railways" was thrown out the window, and plans for the privatisation of British Rail were put in motion.

The resulting Railways Act of 1993 was nothing short of a fire sale, and instigated the atomisation of Britain's formerly unified railway. Dozens of new private entities were created, with the process concluding by 1997, prior to the next general election. The ensuing period was punctuated by four highly public fatal derailments, all a result of the new railway structure, following which the ownership and operation of the railway infrastructure was brought back under state control. While overall passenger and worker safety had continued to improve through the early years of privatisation, these and other tragedies exposed systemic failures in the fragmented structure of the industry as it had been drawn up by the Treasury. If the first five years following completion of privatisation were about exposing the failures in the system, the subsequent fifteen were about unpicking that system in its (near) entirety. Indeed, less than a decade after the completion of privatisation, the railways were under greater government control than at any time in their history.

Nevertheless, by this point the tide had turned. Railways were at their most popular since the early part of the previous century. Passenger numbers were enormous, and there was cross-party consensus that rail investment and the expansion of the rail network were a good thing. Franchises previously procured as "not for growth", such as those in Wales and the North of England, were creaking at the seams as people turned to trains. The demise of steel and coal traffic notwithstanding, rail freight was booming.

There was a problem, though.

Just as the industry's new structure had resulted in the creation of the rolling-stock operating companies (ROSCOs), which incentivised a freeze in new train procurement, the creation of Railtrack and its private suppliers had resulted in a freeze in recruitment across the infrastructure domain. A decade-wide gap in skills was the consequence. With the growth in passenger demand came a huge growth in the number of infrastructure projects being carried out, and this skills bottleneck, combined with an industry structure that exacerbated costs by maximising the number of organisational interfaces, meant work was being delivered too slowly and at too high a price.

Cost escalations became unbearable for government in 2017 and resulted not only in the curtailment of the national electrification programme but also in the abandonment of other enhancements across the country, particularly in and around the north of England. Meanwhile, there was a glut of new train orders, many of which were for new electric trains, for which there were no longer overhead wires to power them.

May 2018 was supposed to be the moment that an enormous expansion in capacity was unleashed. New track and trains would enable a great leap in the number of trains running. As it happened, neither the track nor the trains were in place to deliver much of this uplift, and the result was a collapse in the reliability of the system. Driver training couldn't progress, and the consequent lack of trains, track and staff resulted in the cancellation of upwards of a third of services in the South East and North of England, with lesser but still significant effects felt by passengers across the network.

Despite the global pandemic resulting in the collapse of the franchising system and offering a chance to wipe the slate clean, this opportunity was not taken. Vague and impotent talk of a new rail organisation has remained just that: talk.

Three decades after our tale of British railway liberalisation began, how are things looking now? Ridership is back up and still climbing, but subsidies are now among the highest in Europe. Thameslink was completed in 2018; Crossrail in 2022. The Transpennine Route Upgrade is picking up pace, but electrification between Manchester and Leeds is not planned for completion until 2041, an incomprehensible half century since the plans were initiated. High-speed links across the country? Almost completely cancelled.

I would not describe this as a ringing endorsement of rail market liberalisation, but there's more at play. The UK suffers from the most centralised government of any advanced economy in the world. Its institutions are creakingly outdated and hopelessly under-capacity, and it is beholden to "fiscal responsibility" (read: austerity) as classical society was beholden to its gods.

As with every country we'll go through in this chapter, the wider context beyond the railway is equally if not more important than the structure of the railway itself. However, it was not the UK that provided the model for liberalisation across Europe. As the first to break up its state railway company, Sweden gives us perfect example of how liberalisation offers no easy answers for the challenges railway networks face.

In 1988, well ahead of even the UK, the Swedish government directed Statens Järnvägar (SJ), the state rail operator, to transfer ownership of its infrastructure to the newly formed Swedish Rail Administration. The Swedish regions became the franchising authorities for their services while taking on ownership of their rolling stock (via a separate, joint-owned train leasing company). Franchises were let for between five and ten years, providing some level of service stability.

The state railway operator was able to bid for franchises and initially retained around two-thirds of operations. It also retained a monopoly on long-distance services. By 2001, SJ had been broken up into six government-owned companies along functional lines, but by 2005 the Swedish government was still not satisfied with the level of liberalisation. By this point, several of the constituent companies of the former SJ had been peeled off and privatised, including those responsible for train maintenance and repair.

Having one of the most liberalised railway markets in Europe has failed to stop Sweden's railways from facing the same challenges as many of its fellow national systems. The cancellation of critical high-speed infrastructure for political reasons to one side, Sweden's infrastructure has not seen investment keep up with demand, and its signalling in particular is creaking at the seams. Much of it is reaching its expiry date already, and more than half will be unmaintainable by 2040. The poor condition of the track has accounted for several derailments, with consequences thankfully limited to severe disruption.

Operators are investing in new trains, but without the infrastructure brought up to scratch, this won't make any real difference to services. Crucially, government funding of the railways is barely enough to keep pace with existing levels of operation, with no funding being provided to deal with today's level of growth, let alone accelerated growth to tackle transport emissions.

Compounding these problems, and driven by the Swedish government's fixation on creating as liberalised a railway as possible, is the new market-oriented service planning tool introduced by Trafikverket, which initially resulted in much of the Swedish system toppling over when it was first deployed in late 2022. It is still causing problems today. The lack of timetable resilience afforded by its flawed design does not mix well with the private operators continual push to reduce staffing on its services (cheered on, it must be said, by the regional authorities).

Yet the Swedish railway system continues to hang on by its fingernails, driven mostly by significant demand for growth despite its failings.

In the Netherlands, ProRail looks after infrastructure and is funded in ten-year cycles. Nederlandse Spoorwegen (NS) owns and operates the trains. Both organisations are state-owned and are regulated by the Office for Consumers and Markets, which largely focuses on track-access disputes. NS runs almost all rail services under a concession contract that it gets awarded by default by the Ministry of Infrastructure and Water Management, with some rural services being operated as separate franchises under a public tendering process. In those cases, trains are owned by the rail operator.

In 2024 — and in a sign of its total disconnection with reality when it comes to railway operations — the European Commission rejected the latest award of rail services to NS on the basis that the concession was not competitively tendered. Further to this, they postulate that significant elements of the national system could be sliced off and delivered by private operators. The Netherlands operates the most densely used railway network in Europe, and the idea that competition would be anything other than extractive and wasteful is not one worth heeding.

In the words of outgoing secretary of state Vivianne Heijnen: "I cannot leave our interconnected domestic network to the market now. Now is not the time to experiment." She's spot on.

Meanwhile, Ukraine is aiming for accelerated membership of the European Union and has been preparing in accordance with its 2017 association agreement in the meantime. A precursor to membership is the liberalisation of its railway market, the primary consequence of which is the splitting of infrastructure management from railway operations, followed by the splitting of passenger and freight operations and so on. In the words of the 2019 minister of infrastructure Vladyslav Krykliy: "We are laying the groundwork for fair competition, because it is the basis of success." Observing countries where liberalisation is more advanced will allow us to evaluate his assertion, but in the Ukrainian context, despite the scale and success of its operations, the railway system was and still is mired in corruption, with outdated regulation, poor management and degraded trains and infrastructure.

There's no end of papers, news stories, blogs and press releases from before the war talking about the necessity and value of these structural changes to Ukraine's railways. In what I would suggest is a classic trope of European railway reform that can map onto many countries not on our Top Twenty list, a complex series of problems is perceived as being easily resolvable by market liberalisation rather than, say, tackling corruption, modernising regulation and management practices or investing in new trains and upgraded infrastructure.

There is a tragic recent example of liberalisation's inability to prevent corruption from causing tragedy. In 2023, two trains collided head-on in Tempi in Greece, killing and injuring 142 people. EU prosecutors subsequently called for the prosecution of Greek ministers as it emerged that contract manipulation relating to upgrading of the line's signalling system had been facilitated by the state managing authority. This corruption meant that signalling protection was not adequate, leading to the crash. Corruption can threaten or compromise the safety of the railway, and in this case, as in others, we see that liberalisation, far from preventing corruption, likely facilitated it.

Ukraine's railway liberalisation plans have been rightly delayed until after the war. I would suggest that the value of maintaining a relationship between infrastructure and operations that isn't bogged down by commercial barriers is evident in this case, as Ukraine's railways have had to respond to the extreme damage from heavy usage and bombardment since the Russian invasion began.

However, no country better demonstrates the impotence that follows letting private capital run national transport systems than the United States. In the inter-war years, it wasn't a dead certainty that the US would go on to convert its entire identity into one defined by automotive "freedom", but in the aftermath of the Second World War, that's precisely what it did. The rapid construction of the interstate system following the 1956 Federal-Aid Highway Act cemented this decision, allowing highway-hauled goods to dominate. At the same time, the construction of sprawling suburbs — connected to the new highways and planned in such a way that they were very difficult to serve with any form of public transport —

resulted in great increases in the use of cars over public transport, and over rail in particular.

The railroad companies — of which there were 113 major players in 1956 — quickly gave up on goods that were costly to handle, but a lack of investment to compete with either passenger or freight movement by highway meant they were quickly left behind, shedding modal share (that is, what percentage of people and things move by rail versus by road, air and water) to motor traffic. Consolidations and bankruptcy left only 58 major railroad companies by the end of 1976.

That year, Conrail (or rather, the Consolidated Rail Corporation) was formed by the federal government and took over operation of most of the railroad network of the North Eastern US. This was in the aftermath of the collapse of several major railroad companies, the largest of which was the Penn Central Transportation Company. The demise of Penn Central was the largest bankruptcy in US history, and the US government knew that its disappearance would cripple the US economy.

Conrail went about tidying up what it could of the incoherent network it inherited, and within a few years had turned its operation into a profitable one, largely as a consequence of the eradication of restrictive regulations on railway operations that gave an inherent advantage to road haulage. The Staggers Act in 1980 reversed regulation that had been in place to control the monopoly railroads held at a time when they had no competition — ironically, it was this regulation that had contributed to their demise and the rise of the individually hauled truck in the post-war years.

By the middle of the 1980s, Conrail was no longer just profitable, it was successful by the measures of the day, returning piles of cash back into federal coffers. Deregulation was only part of the story by this point, with significant mileage and all of its passenger services having been cut. Passenger services in the rest of the country had for the most part been obliterated by the early 1970s, at which point the federally owned National Railroad Passenger Corporation — branded Amtrak — had picked up most of what remained. On its creation in May 1971, it dropped half of the 360 or so services it inherited, leaving around 180 to be continued.

Of the few suburban railroad systems that had survived into the 1980s, usually operated by private railroads under contract to city or regional transit authorities, several were transferred to the transit authorities to be operated directly. Demand started to rise for these services, as it did for Amtrak, not least on the Northeast Corridor, where investment in upgrades had started to make a dent in the overall mode share.

Meanwhile, a profitable Conrail (which could have cross-subsidised Amtrak and other passenger services) was anathema to the Reagan administration, who finally dumped the company into the private sector in 1987, where it saw continued and increasing profitability.

The precedent of profitability through efficiency set by Conrail was seen as a model to be followed by the rest of the freight railroads, and the theory of precision-scheduled railroading (PSR) was introduced in the 1990s. PSR was supposedly intended to maximise the use of train equipment and track access to increase throughput, predictability and reliability. It did anything but.

Instead, the industry fixated on operating ratios (a railroad's outgoings as a percentage of its revenue) and saw PSR as a tool to deliver this over and above all else. This drove the lengthening of trains without any upgrading of infrastructure to cope, with consequent impacts on the throughput, predictability and reliability that PSR was meant to improve. It meant greatly worsened working conditions for crews, with the level of scrutiny of working hours essentially trapping rail staff in conditions bordering on indentured servitude. It even meant increased numbers of over-long trains breaking apart or derailing, as well as other safety impacts from cuts to infrastructure maintenance or operating scrutiny.

As Justin Roczniak, co-host of the *Well There's Your Problem* podcast put it, the current US railroad system

> is the result of a deliberate, half-century-long conversion [...] from a network that could deliver many kinds of goods to market (while also hosting hundreds of passenger train lines), to a fleet of land barges that are good for coal and containers — not much else.

This is all framed by the enormous profiteering of the major railroads. From 2010 to the present day, US rail companies have distributed $200bn in shareholder payouts, all the while they refuse to invest in upgraded track layouts, electrification or modern control systems. They continue to actively relinquish market share to road haulage, and have stretched their workforce to breaking point. The US railroads are on the brink of collapse.

Today, there are around six hundred freight railroad companies in operation in the US, each owning its infrastructure (but operating over other lines via trackage agreements) and either owning or (in some cases) leasing its rolling stock. Of these, six are the so-called Class 1s — massive operations that account for 70% of network length and 90% of staff.

Attempts to further expand passenger rail services across the US are slow, independent of whether they're led by private or state organisations. Some success has been had in growing urban tram systems, but these cannot drive the modal shift needed to release the USA from its automotive chokehold.

Market liberalisation should not be confused with interoperability either — the advantages of a coherent network of networks are enormous given the ability to move people and (particularly) goods across borders. Conversely, the inability to do this limits the success of a railway system. As with the other Baltic states, Finland's railway system is somewhat hamstrung by its use of Russian track gauge, despite much of its trade and international passenger travel being European. Nearly two centuries on, a lack of standardisation of track gauges is still constraining economies and mobility. The upshot of this is that liberalisation in line with the rest of Europe isn't much use when trains cannot operate across the break in gauge. Hence we see that liberalisation isn't a driver of better railway connectedness; standardisation is, and this is only easier when there are fewer operators and states can compel them to standardise.

Let's look at British trains for a moment, to explain perhaps the most egregious example of the failure of a liberalised rail market to deliver positive change — or perhaps the success of a liberalised rail market in extracting rents.

Following privatisation, three ROSCOs bought — at rock-bottom prices — an enormous range of hugely valuable trains that had been scrimped and saved for over the preceding decades by state operator British Rail. They then leased these back to the train operators at eye-watering cost and with little oversight, enabling a significant outflow of cash (to the tune of hundreds of millions of pounds a year, far more than the profits of the private train operators) from the industry. It's little coincidence that these groups were initially run by consortia of banks and have finances that are funnelled via low- or zero-tax regimes to obfuscate their earnings. This has incentivised one of British passengers' biggest gripes: the common use of trains that are as short as possible to minimise leasing costs, without a care for the level of overcrowding that this results in.

Another impact of the ROSCOs landing a large, cheap asset that they could rent out at high prices was the near death of the UK train manufacturing industry, as there was no incentive to continue British Rail's programme of fleet renewals. In the aftermath of privatisation, only British Rail's partially fulfilled orders remained on the books, and new passenger trains wouldn't be built at volume until the early 2000s, resulting in the demise of all but the Derby works. At great cost, new plants have opened in Newton Aycliffe and Newport since, but these and the plant at Derby continue to teeter on the brink of closure thanks to the lack of any long-term rolling-stock strategy.

That liberalisation fails on its own merits does not mean that nationalisation solves all of the problems of a railway network. Invariably it is just the first step on a long road to reshaping the railways to deliver for their users. To improve further, the countries further down our list need to invest in improving their infrastructure — in each and every case, decay or a lack of capacity is constraining growth.

## 2. Avoiding investment is expensive

Where railway expansion has been most rapid, it is because countries have taken a view of what their future railway systems should look like, not what benefit-to-cost ratio a given railway project might generate.

With emissions climbing, and all the other things that railways can resolve getting worse to boot, now is the time to invest and expand. With power sufficiently distributed and railways democratised, such investment can be rapidly deployed. Forget business cases — so long as there is appropriate environmental and social impact assessment, the worst-case scenario is that a railway remains underused. The likelihood of this greatly diminishes if it is part of a suitably well-developed plan.

We must invest to build the world we want, not dance around the edges of the world we see today, not least as cultures of low investment generally lead to systems that exclude the most vulnerable in society, such as where accessibility changes are deprioritised because the bean counters just don't see it as "value for money".

If we look across the world's railway networks, there is a clear correlation between levels of investment and rail system effectiveness. And the outliers to this prove rather than contradict the rule.

Those countries that buck the trend are the UK, Sweden, India and Russia. We'll look at India and Russia later, but the UK and Sweden suffer from both a historic lack of investment and fragmented organisational structure, in the UK's case exaggerated by extremely dense levels of operation.

The UK, the Netherlands, Switzerland and Belgium have the most densely used railway systems in Europe. I would argue that the density of operations goes beyond correlation and has a causal link to the fact that all of these countries bar Switzerland cannot squeeze further modal shift growth out of their existing railway networks. Switzerland has only overcome this barrier by investing three times more per capita in its railways than the UK (which itself is already high on the list in terms of per-capita investment) and seven times more than the Netherlands.

The UK, the Netherlands and Belgium have only two options. They can either follow the Swiss model and spend eye-watering sums of cash on squeezing every last drop out of the existing network, or they can expand the network with new lines to enable more trains to run without increasing service density. There are no other options. Further liberalisation will only make deploying these options harder, and only the state can provide this level of investment.

Germany embodies this point, and its operating model makes the UK look restrained. In 2021, there were a whopping 630 registered railway operators in Germany, accounting for around a third of the passenger and freight market, with Deutsche Bahn (DB) accounting for the rest.

Liberalisation has done nothing to improve Germany's decaying performance — its problems lie in the condition and capacity of its railway infrastructure. Only now is its government fronting funding figures even close to the level required to drive the necessary modal shift away from motor traffic that's needed for Germany to meet its greenhouse gas (GHG) reduction obligations.

DB is a state-owned company, and is the largest railway company in the world, bigger even than India or China's state operators. It was formed in the aftermath of German reunification and consists of various functional subsidiaries, which are in turn split into further subsidiaries, and indeed some of these are split into further subsidiaries again. In what you may notice is an emerging pattern in the mature European markets, fragmentation is being reversed, with what had been two separate infrastructure operators (DB Netz and DB Station&Service) merged into a single infrastructure manager — DB InfraGO — in late 2023. In parallel with a wide-ranging €45bn investment plan to bring Germany's core routes up to scratch by 2030, this is in response to the biggest problem with Germany's railways: a lack of investment in the infrastructure.

As Jon Worth, an independent rail commentator, put it in an interview with state broadcaster Deutsche Welle,

> Railways in Germany are at the limit. Germany runs a lot of trains on very old and decrepit infrastructure and has simply not been investing in the tracks, the bridges and the signals as much as would be necessary in order to manage to run things with a stable and reliable service.

It's a familiar story. There's not enough overall capacity, and this has a direct negative effect on reliability and punctuality.

This is a problem several decades in the making, too. Following reunification in the early 1990s, funds were simply not forthcoming for the necessary overhaul that Germany's railway needed in line with the massive demand for expanded passenger and rail services. Meanwhile, successive jiggling around with the structure of Deutsche Bahn achieved little — industry structure doesn't change the state of the infrastructure or create new capacity.

There's a lesson here for "green" politicians, too, particularly those in the UK and US. It isn't possible to expand the modal share of railways without expanding their footprint.

It is so often said that the involvement of private companies in the operation of railways or the procurement of new trains allows them to borrow for the future in a way that governments cannot, but this is almost hilariously backwards, and is a line used to mask the fact that restrictions on public investment are a political and ideological choice, not an economic necessity.

Private capital is raised with the expectation that it will make a return at or above commercial rates, whereas governments — even those within a currency union where they do not have monetary sovereignty — can borrow at greatly reduced rates. The oft-repeated adage that publicly owned railways must compete with funding for schools and ambulances is bollocks on two fronts.

Firstly, railways are already almost entirely publicly funded (Japan is an exception, but we'll get into why later), even if it is via a façade of private ownership, and this has always been the case. Turning on the taps of investment is a political choice.

Secondly, public investment doesn't work this way. If investing in schools results in a benefit (say, failing concrete not collapsing onto the heads of your pupils), then the investment pays for itself in economic returns. If your health system keeps your population healthy such that they can keep active and working, then your return on investment comes from fewer people falling back on social security. If a better railway keeps people and goods moving more efficiently and keeps the economy buoyant... well, I've made my point.

On the other hand, what if, rather than building tracks or trains, a government simply created the conditions under which tracks or trains could be built? It's a patently daft question, but it is the one that successive decades of neoliberal transport policy have been determined to investigate. Rather than investing for the future, the hope is that private capital will swoop in and backfill their indifference. But it's a false economy.

The data is rough around the edges and challenging to precisely and accurately validate, but the OECD's data on self-reported inland transport investment gives reasonably comparable figures for per-capita money spent on railways, even if these are at a high level.

The UK spends more per capita than every country on our list bar Switzerland and Austria. That's nearly four times more than Russia, nearly twice as much as France or Germany and thirty times more than India.

Given its relative underperformance, why is this number so high? To a significant extent these high figures are the result of decades of underinvestment now having to be reversed at scale. A network that has seen enormous contraction since the Second World War is now having to cope with very high levels of freight and particularly passenger demand, and that gets rapidly expensive when using a limited number of tracks and trains. Britain runs one of the most intensive services on a largely unexpanded railway system, and there's a cost to sweating the asset to that extent.

Meanwhile, the USA is at the opposite end of the scale. Only Poland, Romania and India (allowing for some data problems for the latter country) have invested less in their railways per capita. When people refer to the Class 1 railroads being allergic to investment, the numbers back them up.

While China has spent similar if not slightly lower amounts than the mid-tier European countries, India sits squarely at the bottom of the investment-per-capita list, spending half what Poland and Romania have in the last two decades. Given the comparatively similar capabilities of each of these leviathan railway systems, it shows how investment alone is not enough to predict the likely success or failure of a railway.

No country better shows the fallacy of assuming recent investment directly relates to success than Russia, which has spent less than a tenth per capita of what Switzerland has since 2000, yet operates (or at least, operated) an immensely successful railway system.

## 3. Accountability must shape structure

To maximise the return on investment and drive increased usage clearly requires the right organisational structure and relationship with elected power at a national, regional and city level. But what does that look like?

We'll talk about the need for long-term planning next, but for a plan to stick requires sufficient democratic oversight and accountability, and this cannot be achieved at national level alone. The countries at the top of our Top Twenty list have strong regionalised power over their railways. Funding and administrative power at local and regional levels is key to overcoming the give and take of political cycles and for pushing operators to do better.

Let's head to Poland.

Since liberalisation started in 1991, what are essentially devolved state operators have taken on an increasing share of Polish rail operations. Polregio is the largest, and is jointly operated by the sixteen Polish voivodeships (regions) as the main local service provider, but there are also several other companies fully owned by voivodeships and running regional services The result is improved responsiveness and local accountability, but it didn't need liberalisation to happen, just a better devolution of railway operations away from central government.

However, as we've seen, devolved structures can provide a smokescreen for corruption and corporate greed if markets are pushed towards liberalisation. Even when their intent is less sinister, privately owned regional operators just create distance between decision-makers and the people the decisions affect.

Romania's railways largely fall under the control of the former state operator and current holding company Căile Ferate Române (CFR), with liberalisation starting in 1998 as the company was split along functional lines just like Poland's were. A number of regional state and private operators emerged following liberalisation, and in 2011, further reforms pushed the system closer to full privatisation, with nearly a fifth of the network being leased to over a dozen private companies who have exclusive use of it.

The largest of these private companies was Regiotrans, and neatly proving that liberalisation is no solution to corruption, this company had its safety licence revoked for almost a month in spring 2015, leaving large parts of Romania totally unserved by public transport. The reason for this revocation was that one or more of its shareholders and executives had been allegedly embezzling subsidies. After the arrest of one executive, another fled to Latin America and committed suicide with his shoelaces in an airplane toilet. The company is still running services today as Regio Călători.

The Romanian government threatened mass closures in 2014, but since 2016 it has been exploring further reforms and modernisations led by a new body, the Romanian Railway Reform Authority. There have been visible improvements, such as new electrification and train fleets, and the number of private operators has been rationalised and consolidated. However, the European Commission's push for liberalisation has not eased, and it is difficult to see that history won't just repeat itself.

In the UK, regional private operators in the North of England have been successively renationalised as they have failed to keep a grip on service quality and industrial relations.

The railways are a system, and splitting them along functional rather than geographic lines only denies the connectedness of that system. Private operators rely on tracks and trains leased to them by other bodies, inevitably funded by the state, and lack the incentive to improve the whole.

Switzerland and Austria are achieving the levels of rail usage the rest of the world needs to achieve, and they have done this largely through vertically integrated organisational structures and high levels of investment. Competing operators are permitted onto the national systems as guests, but the strength in both systems is in the frequency and regularity of services and integration across modes. This need for vertical integration (or reintegration) has not been lost on the mature railway markets.

The French railways have seen successive reforms in recent years, with the latest, in 2020, creating a single state-owned group holding all shares in the five subsidiaries of SNCF, its national railway organisation. This essentially brought France's main railway operator as close to being fully nationalised as the European Commission would allow. Infrastructure manager SNCF Réseau, formerly split out as per the usual liberalised model, is now part of the SCNF group, and consequently the overarching railway strategy can be overseen and enacted more coherently. Autorité de Régulation des Transports acts as the independent regulator to ensure SNCF is not given unfair advantage over other operators, but overall the restructuring has acted to bring railway operations closer together, and alongside a transfer of debt from commercial to state books, it should help reverse some of the decline and decay in the regional rail services away from the high-speed network. The debt restructuring in particular was negotiated while giving greater strategic oversight to the French government. This aligns with longer-term funding settlements and more radical French plans for greater rail usage versus road and air.

Devolution of operation to the regions began in 1997 and was completed by the early 2000s, with ridership picking up alongside the decentralisation of service specification. Under the current structure, the regional authorities provide subsidy and oversight directly to SNCF Voyageurs as the frontline passenger operator. SNCF also holds shares in a large number of companies that provide a variety of functions and services to railways in France and beyond.

The last point to make on structure and accountability regards service segregation. Mixed-traffic railways can be highly effective, as we see with Switzerland and Austria. However, these come at a tremendous operating cost, and create a ceiling in capability. Both countries still have dedicated urban mass-transit systems in their largest cities, and the need for them to expand their dedicated high-speed networks grows more pressing year on year.

In Britain, the mixture of services on the existing network, especially in cities outside of London, means that further capacity is almost impossible to create. It also means that it is very difficult to align devolved operations with dedicated infrastructure, tying local services to national decisions. This is not conducive to democratic control.

The UK's new High Speed 2 railway line was intended to free several urban railway networks of the burden of long-distance services, with fast trains being yeeted across to the fast railway, so we can see how building new national infrastructure can actually be a key component in creating local, democratically accountable railway networks.

This requires an understanding of what service a railway needs to provide and what capacity it therefore needs, and thus requires a view of the future.

## 4. Think holistically, think long term

Our last lesson is that achieving true greatness is not possible by focusing on railways in isolation — punitive policy needs to exist to limit private vehicle usage. This is the case in Switzerland, and for historical reasons it continues to be the case in Russia. Such policies must exist as part of a longer term strategy. The high-performing railway systems we've looked at have detailed plans for development up to 2040 or beyond.

Transport must be considered as a whole, too, and services planned accordingly. This has the benefit that, once a timetable is established, pinch points or constraints on capacity become obvious and fixing them can be planned for.

Switzerland's Federal Office for Transport oversees the whole railway network and is owned and operated by the Swiss Federal Railways (SBB) and two smaller canton-owned operators. These contracts, as well as those run by smaller operators (Switzerland has many integrated narrow-gauge railway lines) are determined in a multi-year consultation process prior to concession awards, essentially to determine who makes most sense to operate each line based on the timetable requirements. Rolling stock is owned by the companies.

The timetable itself, as regular and perfect as a Swiss watch, is planned by a separate organisation, called Trasse Schweiz, which is jointly owned by (but independent of) the three main operators. Trasse Schweiz is a critical component in enabling Switzerland's Taktfahrplan, the regular drumbeat of services from long-distance trains to local buses, which enables Switzerland to drive such high modal-share figures for public transport. Everything is integrated. Connections are easy. Infrastructure requirements are derived directly from the plan. It's brilliant.

This doesn't preclude access by international operators, either: Germany, France, Italy and Austria all run services into Switzerland.

For any effective public transport system, the balance between passenger and freight operations is critical for the long-term viability. The United States has a dreadfully imbalanced railway where the needs of passengers are secondary at best. For this and other reasons, the future of its national network is grim without radical overhaul of ownership and incentives.

Japan, meanwhile, has a radically different railway operating model to every other country in the world, and it's a structure set up to favour passenger operations over everything else.

Where Japan really sets itself apart is that both operational and investment funding comes from the private railway companies. The JR companies achieve this by doubling as property developers in and around their city stations. Smaller companies achieve this through fare income alone.

However, Japan has a chronically ageing, urbanising and declining population. If current trends persist, its population is estimated to halve by the end of this century. This is putting significant stress on rural railway operations, and as a result, the state has had to step in to provide support to an increasing number of railway companies. These trends are partly fuelled by vicious immigration policies and severely declining birth rates, the latter driven by Japan's high cost of living and high-stress working conditions. Without a reversal, significant portions of Japan's railway network will become non-viable and closure will be inevitable.

Railways do not exist in a bubble. Without a consideration of wider policies, we fail to understand their successes and failures. Likewise, without considering railways within the framework of wider transport and other policy domains, we cannot fully harness their strengths.

## The world's Top Twenty railway networks

This list isn't composed based on safety; it isn't looking at comfort or punctuality (at least not directly); it isn't looking at speed, and it isn't looking at size (not in absolute terms, anyway). This is looking at the mode share of rail versus other forms of transportation, and the passenger and tonne kilometres carried by national railway systems. It gives a fascinating insight into the shape and capability of the global railway, and upsets some commonly held misconceptions about which systems might deserve to be held in highest esteem.

Given that transport is the largest source of greenhouse gas emissions in the developed world, and that the figures are rising sharply in the developing world, you would hope that a greater effort would be made at a national and international level to collect, collate and publish detailed, comparable and up-to-date statistics on transport, by mode. Alas not.

To deal with the mixed statistics, I've ranked countries by their combined passenger and goods modal share by rail, and have also ranked countries by the volumes of passenger and tonne kilometres moved by rail versus by road *per capita*. This can get a little messy as the road data includes road public transport, and the rail data (in most cases) does not include urban rail systems like tram and metro. However, keeping the numbers consistent and normalising the figures by population gives a good guide to the capability of a railway system.

To get my final ranking, and to even out the kinks between the two sets of data, I sum both rankings by country and rerank the result. It's as scientific as I can be short of commissioning a PhD into the subject. And it turned out to be a pretty informative exercise.

Sneaking into positions twenty and nineteen are Belarus and Ukraine, respectively. Both of these countries rank very highly in per-capita passenger and tonne kilometres on rail versus road, but they drop down the final ranking as there are no published modal share statistics validating the numbers.

In the case of Ukraine, the data is from before Russia's full-scale invasion of the country in 2022. The Ukrainian railways have very visibly proven their mettle in many ways since the ramping up of that conflict, but even before this, the scale of both passenger and freight haulage per capita was immense, with Ukraine carrying nearly as much freight on rail, per capita, as the United States.

Belarus is let down by also having about double the amount of per-capita passenger and freight kilometres moved by road as Ukraine, but otherwise the two countries have comparably successful rail systems. If modal share data was available, there's a good chance they'd have been a lot further up the list.

Next, we get to four countries with railway systems I'd describe as "underperforming with style": at positions eighteen, seventeen, and joint fifteen on the list are the United Kingdom, the USA, the Netherlands and Belgium.

The UK, the Netherlands and Belgium all have similarly successful rail systems, with the balance of operations swung in favour of passenger operations, but to a lesser extent as you climb up the ranking. The UK and Netherlands shift over three times as many passenger kilometres as tonne kilometres of goods, whereas Belgium shifts around double the volume of passengers to goods (for the sake of this ranking I am treating one passenger as approximately interchangeable with one tonne of goods).

Per capita, road usage for passenger travel is very similar between these three countries, and in fact, the UK hauls only half as much freight by road per capita when compared with its continental neighbours. In terms of modal share, the three European neighbours are again comparable, though Belgium has approximately double the freight modal share of the UK, and the UK double again that of the Netherlands.

Culturally, rail is seen as a public good in Belgium and the Netherlands, and ticket prices are held down to be competitive with fuel costs for driving. Free or heavily subsidised season tickets are offered to public-sector commuters. Being at the core of Western Europe's high-speed network, both countries have the benefit of three international high-speed operators providing links to France, the UK, Germany and beyond.

Why, then, is the United States in among these close European competitors? Anyone with a bit of rail knowledge will probably know that the US railroads pride themselves on being world-beaters when it comes to rail freight shifted. In absolute numbers, the US only ranks behind (spoiler alert) China and Russia in terms of raw tonne kilometres shifted. The trouble is, if you adjust for population, the US's per-capita tonne kilometres start looking a lot less impressive, with Russia, Australia, Canada, Kazakhstan and Latvia beating them by some margin.

When you then factor in that the US has a diminished passenger rail system that, on a per-capita basis, only ranks ahead of Bangladesh, South Africa, Indonesia, Brazil and Pakistan, suddenly the fact of its ranking alongside the low countries and little old Blighty makes a little more sense.

But that isn't the end of the issues with the US's transport system. In absolute terms, only China and India get close to the total road passenger kilometres travelled in the US, and even then, Americans drive 6.6 trillion passenger kilometres a year versus 4.8 and 3.6 trillion in India and China respectively.

The pain really kicks in when you adjust for population, though.

Only Kazakhstan gets close to the per-capita passenger and tonne kilometres moved by road in the US, with more than double the average figure for the other countries on our list.

Thanks to the utter and total dominance of road transport for passenger travel, rail essentially doesn't factor at a national level. Consequently, it doesn't matter that US railroads carry a decent lick of goods. The average American travels over 20,000 km a year by car, while they barely travel one hundred by rail. In other words, for every 1 km people travel by rail, they travel over 200 km on the road.

Next, we move into a cluster of mid-table countries with broadly comparable capabilities that I'd describe as "delivering": in places fourteen to eight, in order, are Poland, Romania, Finland, France, Germany, Czechia and Sweden.

The outlier of this group is Romania, which sits at number thirteen. It has fairly low per-capita rail usage, but it also has fairly low per-capita road usage. A deeper analysis would unpick the relative economies of these countries and identify how much poorer each is versus its neighbours on the list, but independent of any additional sleuthing, Romania is a country that simply doesn't move around as much. Summing its average road and rail kilometres travelled per capita gives a figure that's firmly at the bottom of the list of countries for which that data is available. This can be seen as an opportunity: as Romania's economy grows and mobility increases, its government should direct the increased flow of passengers and freight onto rail as much as is possible.

There's not much separating the other countries occupying this part of our Top Twenty. Broadly, per-capita road usage reduces and per-capital rail usage increases as you climb the rankings. France and Germany have greater absolute road and rail usage figures, but when normalised by population they compare closely with their counterparts. All of these countries have solid modal share figures, particularly for freight, ranging from 15% to 40%.

Next, two very different countries with railway systems functioning in totally the opposite way to each other, and that consequently end up paired in the rankings. In at number seven is Australia, and at number six is Japan.

Australians move around *a lot*. Their total per-capita passenger and freight kilometres are almost four times those of Japan. Consequently, although they move an enormous volume of freight per capita by rail (only being beaten by Russia), they also move an enormous volume by road. And when it comes to passenger travel, Australian railways barely feature at all, with per-capita ridership similar to Belarus and pre-war Ukraine.

Essentially, as one of the world's primary sources of coal and ore, Australia's railways are configured primarily to shift freight. Conversely, Japan's are operated almost exclusively for passengers. Per capita, Japan carries the lowest volume of freight of any of the countries I could get comprehensive data for.

Then what of Japan's passenger-carrying rail capabilities? Even in absolute terms, Japan is third in world for the number of passengers its railways carry, behind India and China. But when normalised for population, Japan's passenger railways are unbeatable, accounting for 50% more passenger kilometres than the next country on the list, Switzerland.

As a large, highly developed country with a hyper-capitalised economy, the dominance of its railways versus other highly developed nations is spectacular. There are many factors at play that contribute to this success, a key one being the fact that, having set up the railway system almost entirely for passenger use, there are consequent benefits in the removal of congestion and a reduction in maintenance and safety requirements due to not mixing passenger and freight services together.

What sets it above Australia is how well it ranks in terms of the overall mode share of rail. While Australia has a 60% mode share for rail freight, Japan's immense 33% modal share for passenger travel sets it slightly above Australia in those rankings, nudging it one place up on our Top Twenty.

There's little to separate them, though. Australia and Japan have railway systems I'd describe as "grossly imbalanced" — to get higher in the list, you need to be an all-rounder.

Enter the "elites". These railway systems are superior in both passenger and freight conveyance simultaneously. And there's not a hair's breadth between them, according to my data at least: sharing equal second place are India, China, Austria and Switzerland.

On absolute ridership alone, China and India's railways are unrivalled. These two countries have railway systems and usage so expansive that they are an order of magnitude greater than their nearest competitors, save for Japan, which still only reaches barely a third of the passenger kilometres of India.

For scale, let's quickly look at what the railways achieve in these countries in terms of emissions savings alone.

On average, railway travel in India emits around 11.5 grams of CO2 equivalent (gCO2e) per passenger kilometre. Road transport in India emits somewhere around 100 gCO2e per passenger kilometre. So in a country that has an annual ridership of over 1.2 trillion passenger kilometres, the railways save over 100 million tonnes of CO2 equivalent (tCO2e) for passenger travel alone. For scale, that saving is around the same as the UK's total emissions from all forms of transport (112.5 million tCO2e).

The story is the same in China, which accounts for around 40% of rail passenger kilometres globally. Passenger rail alone saves 133 million tCO2e.

Switch off passenger railways in India and China, and you would be adding the equivalent of one-half of UK total emissions to the global total. And that's before accounting for the enormous volume of freight hauled on China and India's railways.

Neither India nor China have particularly proactive policies in place to limit road transport — indeed, road usage is enormous in both countries, at least in absolute terms. But they have expansive and affordable railway systems that have seen significant investment in recent years, and the result is that both countries have high rail mode share, with India leading on goods and China on passengers.

China is well known for having built tens of thousands of kilometres of new high-speed railway in only a couple of decades, but its overall railway system has been expanded and modernised greatly over that period too. The volume of goods shifted by rail has increased by over five times since the 1980s. Simultaneously, the number of people using rail has increased over seven times. This cannot be hand-waved away as a cultural preference versus countries in the west — the increase in ridership has been tied to significant investment in the system.

At the same time, India has modernised its railways at an increasing pace since the 1980s, with infrastructure, train and passenger-systems upgrades hauling the massive network into the modern age. Most significantly, Indian Railways has undertaken an enormous programme of electrification via a dedicated, centralised, competent authority, ramping up significantly in the late 2010s to deliver annual rates in excess of 6,000 route-km to modern standards.

By way of an excruciating comparison, achieving this level of annual output in the UK would electrify all of England's currently non-electrified lines in a single year, with the rest of Wales and Scotland being swept up by the following summer. Before this book is published, India's entire 65,000-km broad-gauge system will be electrified with modern 25 kV overheads.

India and China's railway systems should not be seen as similar, however. India's railway network is a significantly older system, while China's has seen significant expansion in recent years, not least in the creation of its high-speed network, which India has only just commenced construction of.

Nevertheless, it says a lot about the durability of the railways as a system that these two enormous countries, accounting for over a third of the world's population, have built and continue to operate expansive railway networks that are as successful as those in Austria and Switzerland, countries that have very small populations (each has less than nine million inhabitants), that are known for running high-precision and well-funded public transport networks, and which each have a GDP per capita many times higher than China or India (in the latter case, Switzerland's GDP per capita is over forty times greater than India's, yet its railway system is no more capable).

Looking again at our data, both Austria and Switzerland operate railways that compete well with other modes, particularly road, with Switzerland having 20% and 46% mode share for passenger and freight rail respectively (these numbers are 9% and 12% for the UK). Indeed, Switzerland has the second-highest per-capita passenger rail usage after Japan. Austria has a similarly high mode share for freight, though a lower mode share for passengers; however, it has a greater per-capita freight usage and consequently a slightly higher ratio of rail to road usage.

It is interesting that neither Austria nor Switzerland have significant lengths of dedicated high-speed rail. This isn't to say that high-speed rail isn't a good and indeed necessary component in a modern railway network — Austria and Switzerland are compact countries with high-density networks offering naturally short journey times and a lot of redundancy for the segregation of different traffic types.

Rather than building dedicated high-speed rail lines, both countries have opted to build high-capacity mixed-traffic lines and invest in base tunnels to reduce journey times by tackling their alpine topography.

Austria's railway system may see high levels of investment, but it also sees high levels of market liberalisation, with its network being used by many operators from across Europe, partly owing to the position of the country as a route from and to the various corners of the continental railway network. Nevertheless, the Austrian Federal Railways (ÖBB) are owned by and operated for the Austrian people.

Austria's railway system relies on high frequencies throughout, and Switzerland takes this a step further by operating a "taktplan" across all public transport modes. This means that speed and capacity requirements are derived from a nationally optimised timetable, and not the other way around, as is the case for most other systems.

Switzerland operates a high-density railway network that is almost fully electrified. Coincident with the scale and coordination of its public transport networks, Switzerland also regulates the movement of goods traffic on its roads. For example, the Swiss constitution specifically directs the movement of goods on key transport axes by rail wherever possible.

India, China, Austria and Switzerland: four very different countries. Four equally competent railway systems. But which country's railway system manages to beat them all?

Yes, it's the Russian Federation.

A gift earned through the sweat and blood of the people of the former Russian Empire and Soviet Union, handed over to the Russian Federation and not yet trashed by its current mob rulers in the way that other nationalised industries have been, the railways of Russia are (or at least were until recently) truly spectacular.

Russia is a uniquely massive country, the largest in the world by area, and in length it stretches almost half-way around the circumference of the planet. With a population less than half that of the USA, this means that it has a very low average population density, so distances are too great to be reasonably traversed by road, leaving rail as a dominant mode for long-distance travel.

Russia's railways have a long history, with the country in its imperial era being one of the first outside of Britain to construct iron wagonways. The size and geography of the country lent itself well to the advantages of rail, and by the 1860s the rate of new railway construction was enormous. In Britain, annual mileage of new railway peaked at less than 2,000 km in the late 1840s. In the 1860s, around the time of Britain's second surge in railway construction, when a peak of around 1,000 km per year was reached, Russia was expanding its railways at three times this rate. At the zenith of Russian railway construction, in the last years of the nineteenth century, this figure had nearly reached 5,500 km, a high mark that would be reached only once more, during the First World War.

In the USSR, annual railway construction never exceeded 3,000 km per year, but this was still an enormous rate of expansion, resulting in Russia's network being beaten in its sheer length only by the US.

In a sign of the relative fortunes of each country's railway system, the US took an early positive view of electric traction and wired up a significant mileage of railway in the interwar years. However, in the years following the Second World War, the US would fall out of love with its railways and massively reduce its investment in them. The opposite view was taken in the USSR, and from the 1950s the rate of electrification was spectacular. By 1970, a quarter of Russia's rail network had been electrified, accounting for over 50% of its freight tonne kilometres. Further modernisation (such as in advanced signalling systems), alongside limitations on the ownership of private vehicles, helped rail build and maintain dominance in intercity travel.

It wasn't a perfect system, and in many ways it was a victim of its own success, with physical congestion on its trunk routes acting as a valve on development for some regions. This was in part a consequence of the strategically planned nature of the network, where the waste of competing railway lines on the same corridor was avoided, but so too were the benefits of redundancy that parallel routes could offer.

Nevertheless, with significantly fewer resources and reduced economic power compared to the US, the USSR built a railway system that was more popular, in many ways more modern and certainly more successful in terms of sheer volume than its Cold War competitor.

A few years ago, if people or goods were moving, Russia was only one of three countries where it was more likely they were moving by rail than by road, with Ukraine and Belarus being the others.

However, our data is not current enough to account for the economic diminishment of Russia as its leadership, desperate to prolong its own existence in the midst of a succession of deeper and deeper economic crises, mounted a full-scale invasion of Ukraine. Until 2022, and despite ongoing economic issues, Russian Railways still exported expertise, equipment and engineering capability to its allies, neighbours and former Soviet Union constituents. Though it is difficult to build up a clear picture at this stage, it appears highly likely that this capability is in retreat as Russia's war diminishes its economic and diplomatic capabilities. Indeed, in April 2022, barely two months after tanks rolled over the Ukrainian border and shortly after Russian retreats from Kyiv, Russian Railways was the first Russian company to default on its debts as a result of global sanctions, failing to make interest payments thanks to the freeze on the foreign currency assets of the Russian government.

The most valuable resource for any railway system, however, is its skilled people, and the war has stretched these resources thin. As Putin's war has ground on, and Russian losses have mounted, pressure to widen the pool of army recruitment has resulted in thousands of staff from Russian Railways being sent to Ukraine, in what amounts to de facto conscription. Further, Russia has seen greatly increased levels of emigration of skilled professionals following the start of the hot war, with railway staff among them. And that's before we talk about the "suicides" of leading managers of Russian Railways that have been publicly critical of Putin's war.

The horrors being committed by Russian troops and leaders in Ukraine and the heroics of the railway staff in that country notwithstanding, the full impact of the desperation and paranoia of Russia's ruling autocrats on an immensely capable and successful railway system is yet to be seen. All the while, the opportunity to further harness that success to cap and reduce GHG emissions in a country of over 140 million people risks being lost. Let's hope enough of the system remains intact, in terms of both physical and human assets, that it can return to full strength quickly following Putin's demise.

In any case, there we have it. A Top Twenty list of railway systems that Anglosphere countries only just manage to squeeze onto, and Australia only ranks so highly (up in seventh place if you recall) because its extractive mineral economy requires railways to function. And the US and UK are in the Top Twenty despite rather than because of their government's attitudes to rail transport.

But what of those not on this list?

You might have been surprised not to see Italy or Spain on here, for example, but private motor traffic dominates in these countries. Kazakhstan has some of the highest per-capita rail usage in the world, both for passengers and goods, but it matches this with high road usage. In fact, for the countries for which I have mostly intact data, even where railways are well used, roads are used far more.

For other countries, particularly those in the global south which do not feature at all, the data doesn't exist to make comparisons, but other sources of information confirm the likelihood that these countries rely heavily on road traffic and do not have well-developed railway systems to compete.

South Korea, with one of the most densely used passenger railway systems in the world, might well have ranked higher, but the lack of associated data prevents me from placing it on the rankings.

Nevertheless, the recipe for success is plain to see.

To really understand why railways must be the future of transport, we have to turn to the alternatives, understand the damage inherent in maintaining the status quo and see through the false choices offered to us instead.

# CHAPTER 1.4

# THE ALTERNATIVES

## Car dominance

If the railways are so good, then why did private motor vehicles take over as the dominant mode by the middle of the twentieth century?

There are a plethora of reasons, but at a fundamental level, the proliferation of consumerism combined with the apex of human resource consumption to flip the economics of mobility on its head. Dedicating a huge amount of resources (one engine and gearbox, four tyres, plus one or more tonnes of metal) to moving one person (or a relatively small load) around suddenly made sense thanks to global, exploitative supply chains. That railways were essentially the most efficient and effective way to move people and goods any distance across land no longer mattered.

Until it did. In the 1960s — barely three decades after extreme lobbying from the petrochemical and automotive industries had changed our language, our streets and our attitude towards mass death (not least of children), all on the altar of the motor car — across the motorised world it was realised that the reshaping of our society in favour of private transport led only to the total flattening of our urban realm, and of the rural realm beyond it.

Today, road collisions account for well over a million deaths a year, and are the leading cause of death globally for children and young adults (those between the ages of five and thirty). As many as fifty million people are injured. While deaths of those inside vehicles are on average reducing, the number of deaths and severe injuries of vulnerable road users such as pedestrians and cyclists is increasing. Road deaths are an epidemic that we have accepted as part of modern society, and it is absolutely appalling. And if we are to accommodate reductions in carbon emissions and increases in mobility mostly through the expansion in our use of private vehicles, whether battery powered or not, then the number of fatalities is going to increase. There is, at best, a paucity of evidence to support claims that driver aids will limit this rise, not least as these are fitted only to the most expensive cars, inaccessible to the majority of drivers.

Meanwhile, the railways are among the safest ways to travel. In Europe, taking the train is equally as safe as flying. Even in countries with worse safety records, rail is still an order of magnitude safer than the alternatives (other than air travel). The reason for this is pretty straightforward: railways rely on a guided system controlled by apparatuses designed to avoid collisions. Roads rely on untrained people in control of powerful and heavy vehicles in an open environment. Cars offer little or no control of the main variable that causes problems in any transport system: human error.

Further, air quality in many cities continues to worsen, even with the proliferation of electric vehicles. The largest source of microplastics in the atmosphere and ocean is car tyres, and this is only going to increase as cars get heavier to accommodate batteries and larger to meet the profit demands of the automotive industry.

Car dominance and dependence have even more egregious secondary effects. The urban realm has been twisted, homogenised, fragmented and flattened to satisfy the needs of these metal boxes. Nowhere is this more obvious than in the US, where whole communities, most often non-white, have been bulldozed to facilitate the growth of highways. Finding somewhere to put all these cars means levelling enormous tracts of cityscape. This is bleakly demonstrated in Detroit, where little remains of its city centre other than acres of open concrete. Head to the suburbs and the construction of low-density housing has resulted in cities built almost deliberately to make them difficult to serve with public transport.

This change to our built-up spaces has fragmented populations, shattered communities and entrenched isolation for hundreds of millions of people worldwide. For the global north, this is resulting in an enormous burden of care as our ageing populations are consequently less and less independent without the mobility provided by walkable cities augmented by good public transport. This results in more reliance on frontline healthcare services, in turn resulting in worse overall outcomes for everyone relying on their nation's health system. No technology can solve this, despite the claims of the tech industry and its coalition with liberal politicians across the globe.

We're a half-century down the line from the first big realisations about the dangers of car dominance, and the need for humanity to limit its resource consumption, carbon emissions and land use has grown catastrophically acute. Thus the need to exploit and expand railways has grown in tandem, even if you also account for our concurrent need to reduce unnecessary travel and consumption.

The reduction of greenhouse gas emissions must come from modal shift from road (and to a lesser extent air) to rail travel. Even with an overall reduction in travel, research from various quarters has established that at least a doubling in overall rail usage is required well before the middle of this century for the UK to achieve even its own emissions reduction targets. The picture is even more stark for countries like the US where only a very small percentage of passenger travel is not conducted by private car.

The energy density of batteries versus fossil fuels means that electric goods vehicles cannot replace their diesel equivalents like-for-like. We will never be able to generate enough electricity or create the required surplus in vehicles to retain existing road-focused supply chains. We have to rethink freight mobility entirely.

Only the significant expansion of rail services, and in turn the railway network, can achieve this. While the running of modern electric trains emits as little carbon as any country's electricity grid, civil engineering work has an unavoidable carbon cost. Strategic rail-construction projects emit carbon in the order of millions or even tens of millions of tonnes of CO2 equivalent. However, this should be compared with, for example, the replacement of a country's private cars with electric cars, which can be estimated to involve carbon emissions in the order of hundreds of millions of tonnes of CO2 equivalent. Meanwhile, each month, in any given country, road transport will emit millions or tens of millions of tonnes of CO2 equivalent, a figure that is not reducing thanks to the proliferation of larger and larger personal vehicles outweighing any benefit from increased electric vehicle take-up.

Further to this, relying on low-occupancy vehicles for transport locks us into highly resource-intensive mobility. Every car requires two tonnes of steel, plastic and, for battery electric vehicles, mined minerals. We may not be able to avoid the use of lithium in our future, but we should not be making active policy choices that increase our consumption instead of reserving its use for where no alternatives are available. Meanwhile, emissions-free rail transport requires no lithium whatsoever.

## Mineral dependencies

The twenty first century and the digital age have seen increasing reliance on a very wide and diverse range of minerals and materials. The tools harnessed by modern society also rely on a number of core components and systems, such as microprocessors, sensors, mechanical assemblies and insulated wires. Interrupt the flow of these minerals or components, and the global economy will start to wheeze within a few days. A sustainable future will require more resilient pathways for their transportation, but also cognisance of the challenges of relying on such a diverse range of base minerals, particularly ones that necessitate significant environmental or social upheaval in their extraction — even after tackling child labour and exploitation.

To lay it out clearly: the future cannot and will not be saved by ever more complicated technologies, because these technologies are invariably resource and mineral intensive. This doesn't mean retreating into caves; far from it. It does, however, require us to reassess the complexity of our solutions and technologies, prioritising those that deploy simplicity and security of resources.

Possibly the most widespread example is batteries: Do we need to include them in every single consumer product? Is it right to be planning for a future that swaps every internal combustion engine with a lithium-ion battery? Should we be developing or deploying battery-powered trains when overhead electrification, which requires far less dubious materials, is only unfavourable because of its perceived up-front costs? Sodium-ion batteries may offer some potential relief, but their deployment is years if not decades from full realisation, even after which they'll always be inferior to lithium in terms of energy density. In any case, until the environmental and social exploitation that keeps lithium cheap is eradicated, companies will not make the leap of faith to sodium.

Over the last half century, the global north has shifted mineral extraction to the global south, where compliant governments allow landscapes to be scarred beyond recognition, workers to be exploited with dreadful pay and conditions, and tax burdens to be swapped for bribes and bungs. Indigenous populations are ignored as the dollar signs glisten.

Not even 20 miles from Chile's breathtaking Los Flamencos National Reserve, and within the boundaries of the Salar de Atacama — Chile's largest salt flat — is an enormous lithium-evaporation-pond facility operated by Sociedad Química y Minera. This complex is visible from space, with the bright yellow and orange rectangles in stark contrast to the greys, greens and browns of the natural salt flats. The scale of this mining operation, one of the largest sources of lithium in the world, is matched by the volume of water extraction it necessitates, damaging the surrounding natural ecosystem and threatening the livelihoods of indigenous Chileans. The small-scale subsistence farming which has trodden lightly in the region for centuries is seeing its irrigation systems dry up, and locals are being left without food or income.

As the greatest consumers, countries in the global north must make the greatest change to their patterns of consumption. Resource demands must be simplified, minimised and as far as possible localised. The less distance a supply chain involves, the more robust it is against climate change. The proliferation of containerisation and globalisation has enormously reduced the prices of goods the world over, but it can be completely unravelled if the pathways of movement are interrupted. And this is precisely what climate change is bringing.

Much of the world's child labour is focused on resource extraction. Whether as casual labour in agriculture or in indentured servitude extracting cobalt for use in lithium-ion batteries, children aren't just suffering as a result of the future we've left them; they are being actively corralled into building it for themselves. Exponential demand for food, resources and cheap labour invariably means exploitation of the most vulnerable in society, and that inevitably means children.

In 2016, Amnesty International reported on the use of child labour in the extraction of cobalt. The cobalt mined in appalling conditions by children as young as six is transferred via a Chinese mineral conglomerate to companies manufacturing batteries for the largest brands in the technology and automotive industries. Apple, Microsoft, Sony, Daimler, Volkswagen, Tesla — these companies are all still selling products manufactured using the labour of 40,000 Congolese children. Around the world, tens of millions more children are being put to work instead of being free to play, learn and live the lives that children deserve to. It is imperative, therefore, that the demand for these materials is limited, and technologies that minimise or entirely avoid the use of batteries are critical tools in solving the climate crisis justly.

Taking a step back, surviving the future means making the most efficient use of the resources we have and minimising the extraction of new resources. Putting rail's immense energy efficiency benefits to one side, it is difficult to get a handle on exactly how much less resource-intensive railways are than alternative modes. However, we can paint a broad and inescapable picture.

Aviation moves small amounts of goods at great speeds, but modern aircraft require a lot of specialist resources in their manufacture to keep them light and reliable, and the airports and ancillary facilities they require are a highly resource-intensive infrastructure.

Shipping may well be resource efficient given the large loads moved with only a single (albeit massive) engine, but low speeds also mean many more ships are required for those goods than if they were moving faster.

When it comes to road, the comparison is clearer. One train can move the equivalent of tens or even hundreds of individual trucks. Each of those trucks requires an individual engine, tonnes of metals, plastics and more besides, all to carry a few tens of tonnes. Likewise — and given the average occupancy of private motor vehicles is never more than two — passenger transport is clearly significantly more resource efficient when using rail.

As each century has progressed, the diversity of the resources and minerals relied on has increased. In the 1700s, mineral requirements were mostly limited to carbon, calcium and iron. The industrial revolution widened these primary resource demands in the 1800s to include tin, tungsten, magnesium, copper, manganese and lead. By the 1900s, the list of core consumable resources had diversified further to include platinum, silicon, thorium, titanium, vanadium, molybdenum, nickel, cobalt, chromium, aluminium and a variety of rare-earth metals.

The mineral requirements of the "renewable" energy transition, alongside the complexifying nature of our technology, has widened this pool of critical elements even further in the 2000s, adding rhodium, tantalum, tellurium, uranium, ruthenium, indium, potassium, lithium, niobium, phosphorous, rhenium, germanium, gallium, cadmium and silver to the list.

As humanity sticks more and more high-density batteries in everything, demand for lithium and cobalt in particular has grown enormously. Pressures on ecosystems and local indigenous communities, as well as the exploitation of child labour, represent the worst indulgences of capitalism and colonialism that people might normally associate with centuries past, not the 2020s.

In 2023, there were around forty lithium mines around the world, concentrated in Chile, Argentina, China and Australia. With demand at its current trajectory, this number will need to rise to as many as seventy-five mines by 2035. Production of lithium has more than quadrupled since 2010. As demand drives prices ever higher, the big players will stop at nothing to dump more lithium onto the market. What impact will this have on the ecosystems and communities neighbouring these mines? And given the majority of the materials are being extracted for goods sold in the global north, to what extent does this rush for minerals represent a new wave of colonialism?

Perhaps a more constructive question is What are the alternatives to just expanding the consumption of minerals?

Research work by Professor Thea Riofrancos and the Climate and Community Project gives us the answer. The difference between the worst- and best-case consumption scenarios represents a 92% reduction in lithium demand by 2050 for the US alone. This is only achievable if private vehicle sizes are limited, numbers are reduced and public transport alternatives are greatly ramped up.

Not all electric vehicles are created equal, and most government policies of like-for-like replacement of internal combustion engine cars with battery electric cars are a road to ruin, so to speak. While an electric bike requires around 0.02 kg of lithium and an electric bus requires around 0.5 kg of lithium per rider, small cars require 1.6 kg and large SUVs require as much as 5 kg per rider.

Meanwhile, conventional electric trains powered by overheads require next to zero lithium in their manufacture. Yet politicians in anglosphere countries, more than anywhere else, are desperate to dispense with the tried, tested and highly efficient overhead electrification that railways have relied on for over a century, instead opting for the use of batteries as a perceived cheaper alternative.

Lithium is only one example among countless others, including refined or processed materials such as plastics, rubbers, lubricants, cement, steel and so on. Not only are such resources finite, but their extraction or manufacture has environmental and carbon implications — significant implications if we think of concrete and steel manufacture.

However, one of our most precious resources is space — the sprawl of human development has fragmented and flattened our biosphere, and this has only accelerated as we have embedded car dependence into our built environment in the last three-quarters of a century.

Making better use of the space we've already occupied and limiting how much more we take up are surely prerequisites of any sustainable transport plan. And thanks to their resource and space efficiency, deploying railways at a far greater scale than today is how we get our space back.

## Things that are definitely not railways

Just off the road to Coyote Springs and nestled within an amphitheatre of Navajo sandstone is a five-hundred-metre length of pipe, briefly newsworthy but now abandoned. To access the pipe you have to turn off the Las Vegas Freeway onto Route 93, drive about 5 miles north and make a fairly non-descript left turn into a wide-open industrial estate. A quarter mile further presents another right turn, with a large, branded sign beckoning visitors into the site.

Today, that sign has a sticker over it to protect the identity of its embarrassed owner, but only a few years ago this sign was emblazoned with the enthusiasm befitting an organisation that had invented a hoover for venture capital dollars. The pipe it was intended to get visitors enthusiastic about had its most exciting moment on 9 November 2020, when two senior employees had what appeared to be a teeth-chattering ride from one end to the other at speeds barely above 100 mph.

Hailed by some hangers-on as the exciting next step in the future of transportation, this was in fact the beginning of the end for the latest incarnation of vacuum tube transport. In 2023 the company was liquidated.

I have, as many of you will realise, navigated us to the world's only ostensibly functional and now former hyperloop test track. Because it is here that we can stand back, scratch our heads a bit and get a handle on why the railways serve as a powerful lens through which to view technologism.

Technologism, or technology utopianism, can be characterised as an unerring belief in the power of technology to advance humanity, and it's nothing new. Its current iteration has been termed the "Californian ideology" and can be traced back to the counterculture of the 1960s, which was agnostic at best about the role of the state. At the same time, the emergence of what would become the neoliberal right, sharing many of the same views — in favour of individualism and a vastly diminished state — resulted in a subconscious alliance in the minds of many policy and tech industry leaders of the 1990s and 2000s. Alongside their strong belief in the role of individual over collective prosperity, they viewed technology as an infallible force for good and believed that any problem could be overcome if the tech industry was given the space to solve it.

Ironically, all this ideology has achieved is the shifting of power away from the state, with its at least nominal democratic oversight, towards large corporations with absolutely no democratic oversight whatsoever.

The consequences have been dismal. Increased consumption and its associated pollution and environmental damage have accelerated climate change despite tech's claim to provide the solutions to global emissions rises. Exposing the contradictions in the ideology, which purports to be about increased freedom, our real freedoms have been greatly eroded as our personal data is mined and exploited for the profit of a small billionaire elite while providing the security state a surveillance apparatus they could previously only dream of. Increasing numbers of people have found themselves exploited as those in the global south are hooked onto the internet and provide ever-cheaper labour, and those in the global north are shifted into increasingly precarious, "gig-ified" roles.

Emerging from this morass in the 2010s has been a renewed energy for reinventing transport systems, and though it isn't a new phenomenon at all, this has resulted in a significant elevation of *gadgetbahn* concepts that embody all of the problems with the Californian ideology and tech-utopianism more broadly.

The term "gadgetbahn" was introduced by Anton Dubrau in 2017, and I define it as follows:

> Gadgetbahn, noun. In transport, novel systems, often speculative, which seem to be infeasible or unnecessary (slang, transport, derogatory).

It is a satisfying portmanteau coined to describe transport proposals that, for all intents and purposes, ought to be delivered using proven railway technology and yet go out of their way to be anything but a railway. Typically, such systems are intended to distract from or come at the expense of investment in proper, functional public transport.

It is often the case that these systems are sufficiently far from actually being built that they get to claim whatever glorious metrics of cost, capacity and energy-efficiency they like. But taking even slightly more than a cursory glance provides plenty of examples to counteract their bullshit.

We'll come back to hyperloop, but since we're already in Las Vegas, let's take Elon Musk's Loop (this is different to hyperloop and should not be confused with it) as the first in a pair of examples that accompany each other deliciously, exposing the problems inherent in these Definitely Not A Railway schemes.

To find the second, we have to cross the Atlantic and visit the university city of Cambridge back in 2020, as then Conservative mayor James Palmer was taking his personal vanity project from pitch to planning. That project? A tunnelled bus system, bizarrely named the Cambridgeshire Autonomous Metro, or CAM for short, which promised to transform transportation in the region. Interestingly, it wasn't limited to Cambridgeshire, wasn't autonomous, and certainly wasn't a metro. But more on these minor details in a moment.

Meanwhile, back in Las Vegas, 2020 saw Elon Musk's aptly named Boring Company nearing the end of its initial construction phase of the Las Vegas Loop. Originally proposed as a tunnelled rapid-transit system using platoons of autonomous people movers, we now know that it is little more than a lane of traffic buried underground, with a fleet of regular Tesla taxis shuttling a few people between stops. Even the much-celebrated autonomy has been dropped, with each vehicle requiring a permanent driver. And the capacity of this system? Merely a fraction of the promised figures.

Even in 2020, various planning applications and announcements had exposed the underwhelming nature of a system that tech and other journalists were still fawning over. Loop gives us a useful bit of foresight as to what happens when the glamour of a technology-heavy solution pushes the rather more mundane matters such as "How many passengers will it carry?" or "Will it actually work?" to one side. As I've heard it neatly put, "Nodes before modes" — in other words, understand what a transport system needs to do and then pick an appropriate type of system that fits, not the other way around.

Looking at CAM, we can see how these proposals typified the opposite approach. Even the name itself was all about technological whizzgiggery. In the technical documentation that was released before (spoiler alert) its demise, there were only passing references to the system's potential autonomy. For example: "CAM presents the opportunity to adopt rapidly emerging autonomous vehicle technology," despite it not being "dependent or in any way predicated on autonomous operation". Furthermore, its "autonomous" features were further undermined by the fact that "driver costs are included, as CAM is expected to operate with drivers on 'day one' and move towards autonomous operation at a future date" — hardly a ringing endorsement.

So it wasn't autonomous. What about the metro claim?

In the UK, the term "metro" has had its meaning substantially diluted over the years and is used to refer to anything with fixed infrastructure (Manchester Metrolink is not a metro, neither is the West Midlands Metro). Globally, "metro" refers to segregated public transport infrastructure that has a system capacity greater than 10,000 passengers per hour per direction (pphpd) — or 20,000 pphpd according to some authorities. This invariably requires a railway system, i.e., steel wheels on steel rails. In the UK, the only true metro system outside of London is the Tyne and Wear Metro, and even this stretches the definition (it is not entirely segregated, and its system capacity is only marginally above the 10,000 pphpd mark). By comparison,

London's Elizabeth line (formerly Crossrail) has a system capacity of 36,000 pphpd.

To work out the system capacity CAM was likely to achieve, we need to dig into the details of the proposal a bit. As is common with urban transport networks, CAM was formed of several branches feeding into a higher-density core. Twelve services per hour in each direction were proposed to operate on the branches, resulting in thirty-six services per hour in each direction through the "core" city centre section. That's incredibly intensive. Modern tram or other light urban transit systems don't often exceed 16 trains per hour (tph), and only in 2018 was London Underground's Victoria line upgraded to manage 36 tph (making it one of the highest-frequency metro systems in the world).

To make comparisons between CAM and a tram, we have to assume what vehicles they each use. For CAM, I'll use the Irizar ie tram, which is the same vehicle that was favoured in the CAM documentation. It's basically an expensive bendy bus designed to resemble a conventional tram. (Interestingly, in the last guffaws of the system before it evaporated with James Palmer's political career, these buses had evolved into naff little pods, but we'll ignore those for now, as they make the system seem even more stupid.)

For our comparator tram vehicle, I am going to use the CAF Urbos 3, a light-rail vehicle used by many modern tram systems worldwide. It follows a fairly common design and is easily capable of dealing with narrow or steep streets. The Urbos 3 also doesn't have to lunk its own power supply around, so it's 50% lighter on its axles than a bus, despite having a 60% higher passenger capacity — unless its operator has decided to ruin this advantage by including batteries in the specification.

These two vehicles give us a maximum system capacity for the proposed network. Looking at the high-density core, CAM gives a capacity of 5,580 pphpd. A tram with the same service pattern would give 9,000 pphpd. With a capacity around half that of the Tyne and Wear Metro, CAM decidedly is not a metro system.

That alone wasn't a reason to dismiss the proposals, though.

If we are going to assess the value of using "trackless" (i.e., tarmac-only) bus-trams, we need to consider the annual tonnages that the infrastructure would have to sustain to deliver the service specification.

Just as I do in my day job when deciding how tough a railway needs to be, we measure this in equated million gross tonnes per annum (EMGTPA). Through its core, CAM would have reached an annual tonnage of 4.8 EMGTPA.

Edinburgh's tram system has an annual tonnage of just under 2 EMGTPA, and other systems have figures up to 4 EMGTPA. To put it another way, if annual tonnages are at 2 EMGTPA or above, then the whole-life cost analysis generally favours steel wheels on steel rails.

Steel on steel also gives significant energy efficiency benefits, as does the increased passenger capacity and reduced complexity (and thus maintenance requirements) of tram vehicles, particularly if they are externally powered. A conservative estimate gives an operational emissions advantage of around one-third for trams compared to intensive bus-only systems.

CAM's eye-watering project costs — mostly from its required tunnelling — were seemingly palatable because CAM didn't interrupt the flow of road traffic through Cambridge city centre. The unit cost of £300m per mile (in today's money) is as much as London's Crossrail project ended up costing, which is baffling if you compare the specification of the two systems.

A small city like Cambridge, with its population of around 150,000 people, may not require a metro system, but its wide and densely populated hinterland justifies some form of mass transit above and beyond a good bus network. Excluding cars from the city streets and enabling a segregated modern tram network would be much quicker to deliver and more cost-effective than a bespoke, essentially fictional system.

In the meantime, removing city centre parking, introducing more rigorous on-street parking restrictions beyond the city centre, and investing heavily in segregated bus and cycling infrastructure would provide congestion relief and better public transport options.

Which brings us back to Musk's underground linear car park, a.k.a. the Loop. On opening to the public in 2021, it managed a peak flow of 1,355 pphpd, and there's no evidence it has exceeded that. Occasionally, local politicians or journalists refer to Loop as a transit system, but it is just a single road lane buried underground carrying Tesla taxis. It's pathetic.

Today, Loop is largely empty. The novelty has worn off, people prefer other means of making the short trips around the Las Vegas Convention Centre, and Musk's reputation has taken a beating since his purchase of Twitter. Meanwhile, short extensions of the system to nearby hotels have been plagued by safety violations, resulting in a raft of injured workers and tens of thousands of dollars in fines.

As Loop opened to the public, back in Cambridgeshire Mayor James Palmer was unceremoniously ousted, with his replacement immediately abandoning CAM, but not before at least £10m of public money had been wasted on it. More besides had been squirreled away by Palmer into a private company intended to oversee delivery of the project and providing a £40,000 salary to six non-executive directors with nothing to do. This company was only dissolved in

2023. Palmer stated he intended to quit politics following his defeat — to which I would say, "Too late; you got fired."

I've chosen these two projects because they capture very neatly the problems with letting technology lead transport solutions. If we can learn anything from them it is to avoid letting the tail wag the dog: a transport system should be defined by its purpose, not by its technology. With limited available resources — skilled people, time, space and carbon being key among them — it is desperately important that solutions are chosen that deliver the maximum benefits as efficiently as possible.

Sadly, politicians being sold (or trying to sell) cars as public transport has been happening for decades. Before being given the kibosh, the CAM had tempted various consultants to embarrass themselves and generate visualisations of what the system might look like, and these laughably trended towards four- or even two-seat cars.

Loop gave us the most prominent recent example, and it was lapped up by the authorities in Las Vegas — with a notable exception being the city's mayor, Carolyn Goodman, who having pointed out that the Boring Company had no experience and that other cities had rejected their proposals, was left thinking (in her own words), "What are we, dumb here?" She was spot on.

Musk's gimmicky attempt to "solve traffic" was announced initially via a promotional video, in April 2017, which included bus-like vehicles (these were later dropped).

His system was to include elevators that would drop these buses — later just Teslas — via a hole in the road down to a spaghetti-like tangle of subterranean burrows, exploiting an infinitely tunnelable geology to send cars from point to point with nothing getting in the way. This idea was as unoriginal as it was illusory.

Possibly the most well-known example of a car tunnel accessed by vehicle elevators is the original Elbtunnel, stretching beneath the Norderelbe from just outside Hamburg's city centre across to the dense industrial docklands south of the river. It opened in 1911 and remains in use, albeit in a secondary role. It is well worth a visit in its own right as a beautiful piece of engineering heritage. Alas, the technology journalists who went starry-eyed when they first saw the Loop video don't seem to have made the trip.

Press forwards a few years and the Las Vegas example of the Loop is operating exactly as a depressing minority of public commentators predicted: it is merely a lane of traffic buried underground between two taxi ranks. We've already described how it carries a vanishingly small number of passengers. On top of this, it has no provision for accessibility needs, and barely any space for passengers coming from conventions laden with all the goodies and paraphernalia you'd expect.

Videos that emerged in 2022 of queues of Teslas parked within the tunnels met with widespread ridicule, more so than the launch videos showing a few Teslas pulling up in an underground concrete box plastered with RGB lighting. Yet its failure has not put off the myriad politicians who still jostle for attention claiming ongoing studies to find somewhere to dump one of these in their own city.

If you want to minimise the initial costs of a system, it may appear to be superficially attractive to pursue these proprietary non-railed systems. Indeed, for limited applications such a system can be appropriate, perhaps in the case of people movers for airports where gradients or other practical limits preclude the application or expansion of existing railed systems.

But if you are going to the effort of creating a dedicated transport corridor, then even a low-capacity conventional railed system will provide an economic payback over the lifetime of the asset. As we'll discuss in a bit more detail later, why choose proprietary systems that only limit your aspiration for the future? Why create something hyper-complicated when a simple solution will do?

Why, in the 2020s, have we still not learned this lesson? Why do politicians keep falling for this nonsense instead of getting on and building what we know works?

The first of the ploys is the “It’s the future” ruse. Spend enough money on the engraved patent drawing, technicolour artistry, scale model or computer-generated renders and people will suspend their disbelief to let you spout your ideas unopposed.

There is no better case than hyperloop. All of its claims of greatness rely on those who bankroll or authorise its early trial projects believing that it is — to use Musk’s own self-hyping terminology when he first pitched the idea — “the fifth mode of transport”.

This isn’t true.

Hyperloop is an extrapolation of linear-induction motor transport — magnetic levitation or maglev to most of us — and this technology is not new, it isn’t even recent. The first full-sized “magnetic river” was demonstrated by Eric Laithwaite in the late 1940s, but viable patents for the technology date back to 1905.

Development of maglev accelerated in the 1960s and 1970s as a response to a technological barrier for conventional railways. At that time, trains were reaching a limit on how fast they could go with the power sources available to them. Japan was already running its Tōkaidō Shinkansen at speeds of up to 130 mph, but climbing above this speed required an enormous additional energy outlay thanks to the increased horizontal oscillations of train wheelsets, known as “hunting” (conic train wheels naturally “hunt for equilibrium” on railway track), that increased rolling resistance and reduced energy efficiency. In the UK, British Rail sponsored Laithwaite to develop novel tracked transport technology as they hedged their bets on the future of intercity travel. I say hedged their bets because, at the same time as Laithwaite was tinkering away, their research department had hired a certain Dr Alan Wickens. Coming from the aviation industry, Wickens stated in his interview that he "had no knowledge of and little interest in railway bogie design". His hiring was a flash of inspiration that changed the course of history.

Following the most expansive and rigorous examination of rail vehicle dynamics to this day, Wickens and his team of boffins identified that effective damping of both vertical and horizontal suspension was critical for enabling higher train speeds without excessive hunting. This research concluded that, given appropriate modifications to rail vehicle design, there was no theoretical limit to the speed of conventional steel-on-steel railway transport.

Laithwaite was allowed to continue his work with British Rail for a little longer (eventually he would roll out his refined maglev system as a small people-mover at Birmingham Airport), but Wickens had headed off the threat from high-speed novel tracked transport for the foreseeable future. The yaw dampers and other improvements to rail vehicle design he proposed were adopted globally, and he remains one of the most important engineers in railway history, right up there with Trevithick and the Stephensons.

Maglev would continue to be developed elsewhere into the present day, but the only high-speed system currently carrying passengers (the Shanghai Airport Transrapid line, using German technology) has been all but abandoned thanks to a more useful paralleling metro line. Japan's superconducting version of the technology is being deployed on Chūō Shinkansen, a line long delayed and greatly overbudget that is acting as a bypass for an already saturated high-speed railway network.

Perhaps adding the vacuum tube to reduce vehicle drag is enough to justify renewed attention to the technology, and even calling it "new"?

Alas not. In the late 1970s, the appearance of maglev technology inspired Rodolphe Nieth to develop the oddly-named "Swissmetro" system, which employed maglev track but buried the infrastructure in underground tunnels — the Swiss love their tunnels — that enabled air to be pumped out to far below atmospheric pressure, reducing air resistance.

History doesn't repeat itself, but it often rhymes. The system's progenitors claimed by the late 1990s to be ready for a test track, but thankfully the reasonably well-informed Swiss Federal Office of Transportation had their doubts. The company that now owns the concept continues to flail around in an attempt to convince people of its merits today. They suffer on in the shade of hyperloop, obscure enough that nobody in the tech journalist sphere thought to draw parallels.

Even hyperloop's bizarre name isn't original, given "Hyperloop Inc." existed as early as 1975, later owned by Lucas Industries, a British company famous for its workers' attempts to take control of the company's innovation strategy (and for giving Ozzy Osbourne his nickname[2]).

Equipped with this context, we see that there's nothing new about hyperloop, and this realisation strips away much of its appeal, or at least it ought to.

The next ploy is the "bait and switch", and it is sadly common across policy domains. In the case of many

---

[2] Ozzy Osbourne and his mother were both ex-Lucas employees. The company was renowned for the poor reliability of its components when installed in British cars, earning it the nickname "Prince of Darkness". Osbourne adopted this stage name as a nod to his previous employer.

gadgetbahn solutions, enormous effort is dedicated to proving how much better the world would be if we only built a new transport system, such as hyperloop reports talking about how transformative fast transport can be, or the CAM showing how much Cambridge and its surrounding environs needs some form of mass transit system.

That's the "bait", and it is often juicy and well articulated. The "switch" occurs when, rather than proposing a known, viable and indeed real solution (say, conventional high-speed rail, a tram line, congestion charging or even just increased parking restrictions), the gadgetbahn salespeople swap out reality for their bespoke, unproven and invariably non-viable solution.

Circular discussions about market demand and fancy technological whizzgiggery can whirr on indefinitely while the key discussion for any transport system — that is, what it can actually achieve — goes unexplored.

We talked earlier about system capacity, and how superior railways are compared to road or other low-occupancy systems ("pods", anyone?). But let's take this further — if you have an enormous untapped market, one that you suggest will be economically transformative if exploited, how is it possible to create that transformation if your proposed system has a comparable system capacity to just running a series of business jets back and forth (or in the case of the CAM, a small bus)?

Well, as a gadgetbahn salesperson, you hope that you can keep your critics busy talking about the snazzy tech for a bit longer. Which is frustratingly easy these days, as a result of the next ploy. This is the "It's tech, not transit" ploy, and it's insidious in today's media environment. Let's head back to Las Vegas, but this time we'll stay in the city centre and take a trip on the Convention Centre Loop.

As we've already described, this thing is a queue of Teslas running in a buried lane of traffic, with a taxi rank at each end. It is no more sophisticated and certainly not more accessible than that. Nevertheless, until its opening, it received repeated, fawning coverage from the vast majority of press outlets (Musk at that point was still a revered character rather than the world's second-most-divorced transphobe). Why though, when from the outset it was so transparently useless? When the first video landed, back when the vehicles weren't Teslas but glass boxes with wheels and seats, it looked ridiculous to anyone with the slightest understanding of geology, tunnelling or transit.

The trouble is, those weren't the people who were writing millions of words of search-engine-optimised copy to be lapped up and drive advertising clicks. Even those news sources less reliant on clicks rarely employ specialist transport journalists nowadays, whereas they invariably will have technology journalists. Consequently, those interrogating these proposals are ill-equipped to appreciate why they won't work, and certainly don't have the understanding to ask challenging follow-up questions even if they do manage to land an inadvertently probing query.

Google "hyperloop news" and even today, as the technology sucks its last partial vacuum-inducing breath, you'll have to sift through pages and pages of articles before you might have the luck of finding a piece written by a transit writer.

This ploy only works until the gadgetbahn in question starts operating, when — in the rare cases that one does — the coverage suddenly becomes a lot more insightful, as journalists ride the system in question and experience how much worse it is than, for example, a normal subway train. However, the point of these systems is rarely to deliver anything physical.

Of our various fallacies, the next is probably the most historically resilient, given it has been dogging advocates for electrified railways since the 1920s at least — it's the "What if we're wrong?" ploy.

In the UK, a country with significantly less railway electrification than the rest of Europe, a session of the Transport Select Committee back in 2020 was instructive. In challenging a witness, the chair of the committee said approximately the following: "But isn't there too much focus on electrification? Do we put all work into electrification when new tech is around the corner?"

What's funny about this is that the UK has uniquely avoided instigating a rolling programme of electrification for decades. The first call for this came in the 1910s as Irish railway engineer Henry Eoghan O'Brien challenged the orthodoxy of steam traction to the extent that he eventually lost his job over it. Successive and increasingly detailed reports looked again and again at whether there were better alternatives to conventional electrification, and time and again the reports concluded that, no, there were not.

In 2019, Network Rail (the state organisation that manages most of Britain's railway infrastructure) was commissioned to write yet another of these: the Traction Decarbonisation Network Strategy. It was so thorough and decisive in its determination that conventional electrification was the only long-term solution for Britain's densely used railways that the Department for Transport told them to stop working on the report, and the team working on it was disbanded. Thankfully, someone leaked the interim document for everyone to see.

Back in 2007, a similar exercise was undertaken by the UK Government as part of a drive to decarbonise rail transport. They concluded that electrification was not the right approach given the potential for new technologies.

Nearly two decades on from this and neither battery nor hydrogen trains are providing anything but fringe applications, and none are currently running in fleet service in the UK.

I use the example of electrification because it is one for which all the evidence, right down to the basic fundamentals of physics, shows why there will never be a more efficient technology, and yet the UK, the US, Australia, Canada and other countries still push back on just getting on with wiring up their railways. A succession of "studies" in the US in particular have been used to justify avoiding wires in favour of hydrogen and battery trains, neither of which are efficient or cost-effective over their lifetime, for the most part because wiring requires an initial capital outlay that is deeply unappealing to the Class 1 railroads and state departments of transportation. We've had a century of waiting for the next thing to come along; meanwhile, the opportunity costs of running less-efficient, dirtier and lower-capacity railway systems relying on diesel continue to mount.

Our last sleight of hand is a fun one. It's the "AM versus FM" ploy: that's "Actual Machines" versus "Fucking Magic".

Public transport, real engineering, vehicles, in short anything that actually exists has to do so within the AM world: it's messy, it's full of compromises and it costs money up front to get it to work. Meanwhile, in the world of politics and tech utopianism, it is very easy to get proposals that are decidedly fictional pretty far along. This is true across policy domains — in the UK, there is a political agreement across both main parties that, rather than address the chronic underfunding of social care, which is applying enormous pressure to the National Health Service, it is in fact "reform, innovation and artificial intelligence" that will reverse the upwards trend in waiting times and the haemorrhaging of staff. This is Fucking Magic.

The same applies to climate solutions that include any form of carbon scraping from the atmosphere — it sounds like a wonder solution, because it is Fucking Magic. Likewise any plan for the future of transport that relies solely on the conversion of all road vehicles from internal combustion to battery electric: Fucking Magic.

As the gravity well of perceived economic importance has shifted away from finance over the last two decades, an ever-greater overlap in ideas and personnel between politics and the tech industry has only exacerbated this realm of fantasy. When it comes to novel proposals in transport, the advantage that all gadgetbahn and other "new" solutions have is that they don't exist other than in renders and the press copy that their salespeople come up with. They've not had to rub up against the real world. Meanwhile, real transit solutions have existed for decades and centuries, and all of their challenges (mostly political rather than technical) have been visible to everyone for decades and centuries too.

But what is the problem? Surely the due process of our liberal institutions means that, even if a proposal is fanciful, it will eventually be dismissed by our technocratic planners in favour of real solutions? What's the harm in people having grandiose visions of the future? Why shouldn't Marvel put a hyperloop in Wakanda?

Well, if you focus on flashy FM proposals, this provides the perfect reason to delay, pause or cancel real public transport solutions. In a fawning 2015 biography, Musk admitted to the author that his hyperloop creation was not intended to be built; rather, it was specifically intended to derail California's high-speed rail project by suggesting to legislators they'd made the wrong choice in approving it. "With any luck, the high-speed rail would be cancelled."

Battery or hydrogen trains don't work for fast, frequent or freight railway services, but on the off-chance that the physics will change, politicians refuse to commit to sticking wires over the railway. Cambridge still doesn't have a tram line. Las Vegas doesn't have a metro.

Public transport does not need invention. Just like potable water and electricity generation, we've solved the technology challenges for urban and long-distance transport. It is the political will, not technological capability, that is lacking. We don't need invention; we need implementation.

It isn't just for big, highly visible transportation proposals that this is true. The late 2010s saw a surge in the people trying to sell "mobility as a service" as a revolutionary concept. Mobility as a service supposedly describes free-flowing travel across modes, paid for easily through your phone or possibly through subscription, and which is adaptive to your own personal needs. Some of its loudest supporters were those in the automotive industry pushing their autonomous-car technology, and gig-economy taxi companies like Uber.

Of course, "mobility as service" can equally apply to any journey where you walk to a station, hop on a train at your own leisure, change trains (again relying on high service frequencies for quick interchange) and walk to your destination. This doesn't require a dedicated technology provider — letting Google Maps tap into public transport operators' open data feeds gives you all the information you need to string your journey together, and it is politics not technology that would prevent you from paying for the whole journey in one go via a single contactless transaction.

This example gives a peek behind the curtain. Novel solutions in transport are invariably intended to benefit the incumbent powers in transport, namely the automotive and aviation industries. High-speed rail is known to decimate the mode share of aviation, and the success of high-speed rail has squeezed the industry hard in places like France, Spain and the Low Countries. Partly in response to this, but mostly to provide lobbyists with a bargaining chip to prevent more countries imposing reduction targets on the number of flights, the aviation industry has resorted to fabricating nonsense to pretend it can be carbon neutral. Carbon offsetting is essentially fictional; it is an FM solution intended to make people feel better without achieving any meaningful change. Worse than this is the pitching of sustainable aviation fuels as a pathway to carbon-neutral — and unreduced — flights.

Sustainable aviation fuel may as well count as a gadgetbahn given it either assumes near infinite volumes of farmland for biofuel stock or relies on impossibly costly and technically fanciful carbon-capture solutions. The unassailable truth is that aviation is likely to account for a full fifth of human carbon emissions by 2050 — only demand reduction can make a real dent in those numbers.

Meanwhile, the automotive industry is desperate to keep selling new cars at increasing rates despite the obvious and calamitous problems this causes. Autonomous car technology will never work — rather, there will never be driverless cars — but suggesting there might be is enough to distract local and national politicians from introducing congestion charging, reducing parking availability, adding bus lanes or otherwise returning street space back to non-motor traffic. The key question to ask of any novel solution, whether inventive or innovative, is "What problem is this solving?" In most cases, it's not one that benefits travellers.

## Proprietary stupidity

Padova is a fine, interesting city. Though most tourists probably know it as the cheap place you go to stay when visiting Venice, it is lovely on its own merits, particularly if you are a fan of architecture and large hunks of aged parmesan.

It is a university town, with the University of Padova being one of the oldest in the world. Students represent almost a third of the population of the overall city.

Padova is also significantly industrialised, with its eastern flanks now one of Europe's largest industrial zones, multiple times the size of the old town.

This combination of high tourist value, high student population and high levels of commuting means a lot of people want to move around the city. The confined (and thankfully mostly traffic-free) nature of the old town — occupying a significant space in the centre of the city and in the path of most journeys across it — means that mass transit is a critical component in keeping the city as vibrant and economically active as possible.

Given its size — around a quarter of a million residents — the city is well suited to a tram system. And in 2007, that's what they got, thanks to a consortium including Lohr Industrie.

Or did they? If the branding of the system is to be believed, it is indeed a tram. However, a glance under the side-skirts of the vehicles and at the roadway reveals that the branding is fibbing: the "trams" are supported on rubber tyres, and the single steel rail running along the middle of the lane only acts as a guideway. Nobody should be fooled by the length of the vehicles and the pantograph sticking up into the air: this isn't a tram at all. It's a bus. A long, expensive, fancy bus, but a bus nonetheless.

But if it looks like a tram, many of you might think: So what if it has rubber tyres?

It's a reasonable question. The locals seem to use the system a lot, and it has well-built stations that enable level boarding.

But this masks the fact that the Padova guided bus system has fundamental issues that get to the heart of why specification is important, and all of these relate to the lack of steel wheel on steel rail.

The big one: capacity. Increase the frequency of service and the infrastructure, even when reinforced as in Padova, crumbles to bits.

The mass of the vehicles is conveyed on the wheels. And the guideway means that the wheels are in pretty much precisely the same place on the road for every vehicle passage. For a system with steel wheels on steel rails, this is fine, as the principle of load transfer means these heavy loads are distributed down into the roadway via the track system. For rubber tyres on tarmac, though, this many passages of wheels over the flexible road surface would ideally be distributed by the normal variation of vehicles within their lane to avoid the accelerated degradation and breakup of the surface.

This is exactly the opposite of what the guideway does. By locking the vehicles to the same precise path, those wheels run along the same line on the tarmac over and over and over again, sinking into it, stretching it, hammering it and breaking it apart.

Limiting the rate of this degradation also limits the number of services running on the line to no more than about ten an hour, and for a fairly short vehicle when compared with modern tram systems. Limited frequency means limited capacity. The system capacity of the Padova guided bus is no more than 2,000 pphpd, which a reasonable bus service can achieve without the additional infrastructure.

For much of the length of the route, the path of the wheels has been augmented, at significant additional cost, by a reinforced roadway. Even with this addition, the current frequency of service (up to nine services an hour) is causing the road surface to break up, resulting in regular closures and costly repairs.

The consequence of the extra reinforcement was that the cost of the Padova Translohr installation ended up being around €115m in 2024 prices. The cost of the tram project that Lohr Industrie and its consortium partners beat to win the contract? €115m in 2024 prices. As with CAM's later development stages, it's odd how often these gadgetbahn systems end up costing the same as the systems they claim to be cheaper than.

Given that this system has almost all the infrastructural features of a tram has, including overhead electrification, the only ostensible saving is in the cost of laying one extra rail, which, given the heavy maintenance the roadway requires, has been shown not to be a saving at all.

What other shortcomings does the system have?

Let's talk energy efficiency. The larger surface area and higher coefficient of friction of rubber wheels result in about ten times the rolling resistance of steel wheels on steel rails. This means that, though it uses about the same energy to accelerate (50 Watt-hours per passenger), it requires ten times as much to cruise (100 Watt-hours versus only 10 Watt-hours per passenger for conventional trams).

Sadly, nobody has published a rigorous direct comparison of the energy efficiencies of rubber versus steel systems (i.e., buses versus trams), but the above numbers should make clear: it isn't better.

How about ride quality? Having been a willing passenger on the Padova Translohr, I can confirm what the general consensus is for these systems where they've been deployed. Comfort is no better than a regular bus. It bounces around and bumps hard over the various cracks it has inflicted on the road surface carrying it.

Safety? Operators have suggested that the Translohr guideway has a tendency to cause derailments due to its design. Before the formal service started, five derailments took place on the Padova system. This isn't a complete picture, and is reasonably anecdotal, but it doesn't line our fancy bus system up well against its steely competitors. This is all compounded by a further problem, however.

That problem? Translohr, the Bombardier Transport sur Voie Réservée, or TVR, and other non-railed mass transit systems are proprietary. The key characteristic that enabled the rapid proliferation of rail systems across the globe and which continues to enable freedom of choice for transport authorities procuring new systems has been designed out of existence in the name of... making a worse system to lock in a perpetual income source?

By going for this system over standardised urban railway technology, the Padovan authorities have locked themselves into a single supplier. Want to repair or expand the system? With one organisation holding the copyright for the system specifications, they can charge what they like, and if they cease operation, you're stuck.

Conventional tram systems? You can get anyone to lay the tracks. You can buy trams from anyone. You don't need to hoard spares for a dying technology in order to keep people moving in your city.

Incidentally, both Translohr and the TVR systems are now owned by Alstom. The latter system has been essentially discontinued thanks to similar guideway issues as Translohr. And only those unwilling to replace their existing Translohr lines are considering further procurement. Otherwise, nobody is seriously interested. In any case, rail-guided busway technology is now monopolised by one company, globally.

Another consequence of this monopolisation is that it delays the expansion of these systems: only one supplier means a slower pipeline for delivery. Translohr's failings have delayed expansion in Padova, and where other systems have been ripped up, Padova are sticking with it.

By not procuring an off-the-shelf tram system, Padova's public transport system is now hobbled with a low-capacity line they cannot easily grow and which costs significantly more to maintain than a conventional tram.

Decision-makers at all levels must always ask what problem a proprietary system is solving. Translohr is a classic example of a technology in search of an application that it will never find.

Meanwhile, conventional tram systems have seen a remarkable renaissance since the late 1970s. Having been pushed to one side by buses and then by the proliferation of the car, trams reinvented themselves by harnessing the powers of permanence. Combining longer and more-accessible tram vehicles that resemble trains more than the original streetcars, modern control systems and segregation from traffic, these systems, often referred to erroneously as light rapid transit, have enabled the transformation of city centres away from car dominance and have brought significant modal shift back towards public transport.

Thanks to their non-proprietary nature, they can be expanded relatively easily: trains can be provided by any manufacturer, and unlike buses, the modern implementation of trams naturally deprioritises motor traffic and offers opportunities to improve the urban realm for those walking and wheeling.

Proving my point about commonality of systems, many of the most successful tram networks operating today are a hybrid of modern additions and original trackwork dating back to before the turn of the last century. It's a terrific example of the brilliance of railway systems, and as an example of how railways make the world feel. Most people agree that cities with trams just look, feel and run better than those without.

## The frontiers of capitalism

Capitalism has always sought new frontiers — the transatlantic slave trade was a new frontier for generating immense wealth; the Industrial Revolution created a new frontier in the manufacture of goods and therefore profit at hitherto unimaginable scale; financialisaton, the age of the internet, automation and machine learning all represent new frontiers of wealth and income for the capitalist economy.

Another frontier was the literal one created as European settlers expanded their landholdings in North America at the expense of indigenous populations. In the same corner of Nevada we've already discussed above, the Nuwuvi and Newe peoples (among many others) were marginalised as the San Pedro, Los Angeles and Salt Lake Railroad brought in settlers who took on increasingly large plots of land for agriculture. By the 1930s, another frontier was opened up by local business owners and the American mafia in the form of Las Vegas's now (in)famous gambling industry, responding to a demand for entertainment on the part of the workforce building what is now the Hoover Dam.

Roll forwards to the 2010s, and the Las Vegas authorities took a gamble on two Musk-adjacent ventures perceived as being on the cutting edge of a new frontier in transport systems: the Boring Company's Loop and Hyperloop One (later Virgin Hyperloop, later Hyperloop One again).

We've talked plenty about Loop, but let us now talk in a bit more detail about hyperloop. Hyperloop has been particularly effective in sapping public research funding, journalistic attention and administrative capacity. Accordingly, these tech bubbles end up being vehicles for the weirdest genre of guys to write empty books, dominate search engines and earn a speaker's fee at Davos. All the while, either through stupidity or malice, these buffoons do as much damage as possible to the chance of real public transport solutions being implemented.

Off the bat, let's sink this ship. Hyperloop fails on four fronts: capacity, corridor, complexity and cost — the four Cs, if you like.

We've already talked about capacity at great length. We can use the equations of motion to work out the minimum safe distance between "pods": at speeds of 600, 700 or 800 mph, and assuming an emergency deceleration that doesn't turn everyone inside the pods into paste, you need a separation of around forty seconds. Add a little bit of technical tolerance to this, say an additional five seconds to account for the delay between a problem being identified and the brakes being applied, and you see that you can squeeze around ninety pods through a tube per hour. This is outlandish, but let's give them the benefit of the doubt.

If the mock-ups are anything to go by, these pods have around 20–30 seats in them. Again, let's go with the high number. System capacity is hourly frequency multiplied by vehicle capacity, so that gives us 2,760 pphpd. For comparison, high-speed lines around the world happily reach figures more like 10,000 pphpd or even 20,000 pphpd.

Therefore, to achieve the same capacity as a single high-speed line would require eight hyperloop tubes *in each direction*. That's sixteen tubes. Which leads us onto the corridor problem: hyperloop is beholden to the same rules of physics that any railway is, and so it can only maintain those high speeds with very shallow curves. For our example hyperloop system, the minimum curve radius is

40 km, which is essentially dead straight. Nowhere in the world, not even the Saudi desert, will tolerate a straight line of sixteen three-meter-diameter tubes tearing through the environment like something out of Thunderbirds. Interchanges between routes would make Spaghetti Junction look like an Anne Truitt sculpture.

This then leads us to complexity — not a single company "pursuing" hyperloop is considering bored tunnels. All of them are basing their proposals on above-ground elevated structures, partly to allow them to weave some mythos around funding the scheme by selling air rights and powering it with solar panels. This means that the problems of a novel, never-built proprietary system combine with those of a continuous viaduct requiring the design of countless support foundations. This is not a recipe for success, or cost-effectiveness. Because even building a pair of these tubes will be more costly than a conventional high-speed line, and for that pair of tubes you get a capacity similar to a reasonable bus service. The cost of building the system to deliver high-speed rail-level capacities, with 50 metres of pipes bulldozing a straight line through your built-up area, are so laughable as not to merit analysis. And that's before we talk about the stations or interchanges, wherever you'd be able to fit them, not to mention the pod-storage and maintenance facilities, or the pods themselves, of which you'll need thousands, each with near perfect reliability. Or the vacuum pump facilities stretched along the length of the route, multiplied by sixteen, again requiring 100% reliability.

I think you'll agree, this is such a poorly thought-through idea that it ought not to feature in the pages of science fiction, let alone be discussed in the real world. Yet here we are, in a world where the European Union has spent (or torched, depending on your point of view) upwards of €55m on the various scattered companies pretending that hyperloop is real.

Of the fifteen hyperloop companies that I can find, only eight have created anything material. Between them, there are five mini-scale mock-up pods and four mini-scale test tracks. Only the Nevada test track is full sized, and it ran only one human test, reaching the dizzying speed of 107 mph. For comparison, I've genuinely reached half that speed on my bicycle going down a big hill.

The one thing this ecosystem of hot air has successfully created is a unique brand of enlightened, entrepreneurial grifters. Brogan BamBrogan, Dirk Ahlborn, Bibop Gresta: they've all gotten rich on venture capitalist speculation in the pre-COVID era of free money — money which they've spent on fancy websites and shiny suits so that they can keep milking the public speaking circuit long after the fantasy they've been peddling has been consigned to history.

These men have no interest in public transport. They have no interest in science or engineering. They are interested in themselves, first and foremost. If they weren't, they'd be pushing for the public transport systems that we have already to be improved and expanded, because the unavoidable numbers show that rail is unbeatable in achieving their purported aims.

Ultimately, these projects were created to scoop up venture capital, and in doing so, to swipe a little public funding where they could. They exploited the enthusiasm and cheap labour of universities to create some bankable intellectual property. They gave automotive, aviation and tech leaders another seat at the table when it came to steering transport policy in the US, EU and UK. Taking a long, dusty walk around the perimeter of the late Hyperloop One's test track, set as it is into a mighty and unforgiving landscape, might well give you the opportunity to consider what technologism actually delivers us: small ideas made to look big.

# PART 2

# THE PLAN

# CHAPTER 2.1

# WHAT DO WE NEED TO DO?

We know that we cannot keep moving around in the same way we do today. The window within which we can make change is closing as each year of inaction passes. Relying on road transport to meet all of our future mobility needs is absurd, as is expecting some science fantasy transport solution to land in our lap. And restricting mobility to limit emissions will entrench and exacerbate all existing inequalities between social groups and geographies.

I've laid out that the most efficient way to move people and things around — and the quickest way to change our patterns and behaviours of movement — is by using the railways. None of the alternatives can provide the capacity, the efficiency of resource and land use, or the opportunity for mass democratic control that railways do.

But today's railways are far from perfect. Their organisational structures are either creaking or are actively arranged to extract value for an elite class without any heed for their workers or users.

How do we take the railways as they exist now, and mould them into the system we need to survive the future?

There are ten steps that will get us there:

1. Set the mission
2. Redistribute power
3. Restructure the industry
4. Create the timetable
5. Map the network
6. Plan for change
7. Build the workforce
8. Harness automation
9. Maximise access
10. Deliver resilience

# CHAPTER 2.2

# IT'S ALL ABOUT INCENTIVES

Nothing is more important for creating a useful and popular railway network (set within a wider sustainable transport system) than setting the right mission for that railway.

Until we can tackle the question "What are the railways for?", they will continue to flail and fail. Flip this on its head: where the railways are set into wider policy frameworks around delivering mobility cleanly and for everyone — in other words, where the right incentives have been set — they will thrive.

Over the course of this chapter, I'll explain how I get to an answer and how it can be deployed.

## Learning from the frontline

Rail ridership — that is, the number of people travelling by train — continues to climb. In Britain, this is despite the post-pandemic collapse of the cross-party consensus that railways were actually a pretty good idea, and despite strikes, slipping reliability, train frequencies on some routes halving... You get the picture.

Why is this? Well, demand is one element: there is enormous, untapped demand in the UK and across the globe for travel by train.

Crossrail, also known as the Elizabeth line, now accounts for around one in five rail journeys in the UK. That's one new railway, fully opened only a year or so ago, replacing millions of journeys that would have otherwise have been by car.

In the US, the demand for rail has been climbing year on year, even accounting for the impact of the COVID-19 pandemic. Ridership and revenue are now at record levels. This is despite passenger rail being embarrassingly sparse outside the Northeast Corridor between Boston and Washington.

Polling consistently shows that there is cross-party consensus that railways are important, with favourability usually balanced between 90% or more for Democrats and 60% or more for Republicans. More crucially, respondents from non-white backgrounds, particularly black Americans, strongly feel that passenger rail is important to them. Reliable public transport, of the kind only rail systems can deliver, is a key component in urban areas, providing opportunities for work and leisure that have traditionally been denied to the poorer, non-white populations in the US.

In Germany, France, Spain and other Western European countries, increasingly favourable rail policies have ridden the wave of and accelerated the growth in rail usage. Passenger rail usage in East and Southeast Asia have broadly returned to pre-COVID levels, with South Korea exceeding its highest passenger rail usage by the start of 2023 and Japan's JR Central recording peaks of traffic above those seen before the pandemic.

Globally, people want to catch the train. But there's another element: incentives — demand might get passengers into stations, but to keep trains moving, even among cancellations and strikes, you need to incentivise staff appropriately.

How people respond to incentives is an interesting subject. Research has shown that, so long as salaries are kept in line with the cost of living and afford a good level of comfort, there's a limit to the extent personal wealth will incentivise productivity. So long as employees have good working conditions, enough income to afford comfort and the free time to enjoy it, they will be more likely to be happy and healthy, independent of their disposable income.

This isn't the only part of the picture, though. As with most workers in the UK, rail worker salaries have not kept up with the cost of living; indeed, the UK's own Office for Budget Responsibility confirmed in 2023 that the contraction of disposable income in the preceding year meant living conditions had seen their biggest fall since records began, in the mid-1950s. This was a contributing factor in the wave of strikes starting in 2022.

Yet, on non-strike days — and despite cancellations, contractions in the timetable and the vacuum in leadership — these same workers kept people and goods moving in increasing numbers.

So incentives go beyond income and conditions — there is a broad if not universal desire to get people on trains, safely and, ideally, happily. The frontline of the rail industry has a clear objective and a collective desire to achieve it, and this acts as an incredibly powerful incentive.

Let's look at the industry another way: What are the incentives for the current railway leadership in the UK?

Their first and foremost objective is efficiency. Not efficiency in terms of the use of existing, limited resources to maximise the impact of rail, but efficiency as a euphemism for the contraction of the railway system to meet arbitrary financial targets set by Treasury.

This is nothing new. Every year the railway apologetically says, "Yes sir, we can be more efficient and achieve these reductions in cost," and Treasury just applies the thumbscrews tighter. This has been going on since before the Second World War, as the Big Four railway companies increasingly had to rely on government loans as their access to capital decreased. While it saw a sizeable capital investment made into trains and infrastructure during the years of the unduly maligned 1955 Modernisation Plan, British Rail achieved incredible levels of cost and resource efficiency under successive years of austerity. With the arrival of the Railways Act 1993 and privatisation, there was little left to strip back. Thus, even if we ignore that "efficiency" is an unmeasurable and constantly moving target that is a poor incentive to drive growth, on its own merits the pulling power of that incentive has been greatly diminished, with little or nothing left to strip away.

What are the secondary incentives? In the UK at least, the rail industry is held publicly accountable against two measures: punctuality and safety. Again, comparison of the relative success of these two measures is instructive.

Safety is a measurable objective which is tangible, has clear causality and can be improved by the actions of staff at all levels. Even over the years I've been in the industry, I have experienced a shift in the feeling of collective and personal responsibility — but more crucially empowerment — with regard to safety issues. Consequently, safety on the UK railway has seen consistent improvement over successive decades, with it now being one of the safest in Europe.

Punctuality is not nearly as tangible — in fact, I don't think the percentage differences in punctuality across millions of passenger train kilometres is a useful incentive at all; informative, perhaps, but not incentivising.

There are many other lower-order incentives that train managers could refer us to, but those are the big three: cost efficiency, safety and punctuality.

While the single incentive of getting people to their destination in comfort and safety works well for frontline staff, and targeted drives to improve safety have been successful across all levels of industry, the dual aims of cost efficiency and train punctuality are weak incentives at best, certainly when considered against the broader societal need for greater reliance on rail.

What measurable objective can incentivise the rail industry and its leadership and allow current and future governments to understand the shape the industry needs to assume, both physically and organisationally?

## The ultimate incentive: modal shift

To my mind, there's a simple answer to this question, and it provides the single unifying idea that everything else — organisational structure, lines of accountability, staff numbers, train lengths, number of tracks, levels of investment, you name it — can be quantitatively determined by.

That answer? Mode share.

The percentage of people and goods moved by rail versus other modes is a known, measurable and targetable value that can be determined at pan-national, national, regional, urban and indeed route levels. Setting a national target, allowing devolved authorities to set their own targets to deliver the national target, and in turn allowing transport authorities and railway managers to investigate and develop plans to deliver those targets at a service level shows us what the natural lines of communication need to be, which steers us towards an ideal structure for the railways.

Mode share targets are also a straightforward objective to bind into law. And there's precedent for doing so.

On 26 November 2008, the UK's Climate Change Act received royal assent. Unlike similar claims made today in relation to UK policies, the Climate Change Act was genuinely world-leading, being the first national legislation to set "a country-wide, comprehensive framework for climate change mitigation and adaptation".

Originally, it set the UK on a legally binding path to reduce greenhouse gas emissions to less than 20% of 1990 levels by 2050, but this was updated in 2019 to 0% of this baseline (hence the term "net zero") in accordance with updated evidence and international ambitions reflected in the United Nations' 2015 Paris Agreement.

This act was not politically contentious — in fact, the New Labour government of the day resisted pressure for more onerous targets and a more powerful auditing process from the then opposition Conservative benches. Generally, the act was met with widespread approval across both Houses of Parliament. It had come about in part because of various campaigns from advocacy groups, think-tanks and academics.

The targets it set were based on widely available evidence, open to scrutiny by all, assembled by the Climate Change Committee (CCC), which is a nominally independent body of experts. The CCC reports on progress against the targets it set both to Parliament and publicly, providing a clear measure of where sectors are falling behind. It has a mandate that is outwith electoral cycles, enabling a long-term focus spanning governments.

The CCC and the act that created it achieve a balance between parliamentary sovereignty and the consensus of evidence and expertise from industry and academia. It isn't a perfect piece of legislation by any means, not least in that successively more incompetent and populist Conservative governments have drifted further and further from achieving its requirements with only limited mechanisms available to hold them accountable. It also fails to tackle the Treasury problem headlong.

Nevertheless, it has established transparency both in terms of the justification for targets and the process by which government can be held accountable. Consequently, policy changes have been instigated as a result of either actual or threatened judicial review. In other cases, inconsistencies in the application of the Climate Change Act have been identified by the judicial review process, which then allows for further targeted campaigning or lobbying for change.

So if the UK wants to, it can set targets that transcend political cycles and provide a framework for holding government accountable. It needn't be a complex target either. Given the latest figures aren't yet available, let's start with the UK's mode share mix in 2019, which for passenger travel is as follows:

Cars, vans and taxis: 84%
Rail: 10%
Buses and coaches: 4%
Air: 1%

For freight (again using 2019 numbers and assuming the figures have remained constant for pipelines, given no data has been provided since 2013), the numbers are as follows:

Road: 75%
Water: 12%
Rail: 8%
Pipeline: 5%

We've already seen that it is possible for developed countries to have passenger rail modal shares as high as 30% or more, and 60% plus for rail freight. However, let us (for illustration, though I also think these numbers are feasible and indeed necessary) propose the following aspirational figures for the UK in 2050, with the required increase in brackets:

Passenger rail: 25% (250%)
Freight rail: 40% (500%)

We'll get into the weeds regarding how you'd achieve these numbers in Part 3, though it's worth highlighting that London has already achieved a 25% public transport mode share and is aiming for this to rise further. In any case, the above mode share values are all that would need to be defined by legislation, which in the case of the UK could be the long-awaited act that brings (Great) British Rail(ways) back into existence.

By selecting the simplest yet most comprehensive variable possible, you can capture all of the other secondary metrics that are no less important. People won't flock to railways if they are not reliable and punctual. They won't flock to rail if it isn't frequent, comfortable, convenient and clean. Freight won't travel by rail if there aren't the services or facilities to provide for the competitive flow of goods, and if rail isn't reliable and cost-effective.

Choosing the simplest measure as the core incentive for the industry to progress isn't anything new: climate change policy has percentage emissions versus the 1990 baseline; health has the quality-adjusted life year (QALI); education has literacy rates. It's a framework for defining policy that works, and it can be applied across other domains as well — so long as you choose the right metric.

## Inaction is an active choice

Despite still basically being a guy who plays with steel and concrete for a living, writing for national publications has enabled me to get the odd invite to fancy award dinners, and I'm not remotely ashamed to say I have a great time enjoying a free dinner in my Marks and Spencer tuxedo that seems to get smaller and smaller each year.

Anyway, as I've gotten older, I've also gotten a little bolder with regard to who I attempt to sidle alongside and constructively pester. In 2023 I straightened out my dickey bow and introduced myself to the then rail minister. In this situation, there's no point telling them they are a twat to their face, as they'll shut down and their minder will tell you where to go. In this particular case, I'd already met and spoken to the minister in question, as he was previously the chair of the UK's Transport Select Committee, a cross-party group of MPs intended to provide a reasonably objective examination of government transport policy. As it happens, he had presented himself at that hearing as being reasonably well-informed and clearly genuinely interested in spreading the benefits of railways beyond the M25, despite his wider politics as a "moderate" Conservative.

So I introduced myself. At the time, the last remains of Britain's long-term rail strategy were looking increasingly likely to be dropped as High Speed 2 got closer to cancellation, and I saw this as an opportunity to press a point home. The minister offered his thoughts, and as I darted my eyes to his special advisor and her glass of slowly sipped water, he brought up the same old adage about different departmental demands on Treasury.

Choosing my words carefully, I attempted to break down why considering different policy categories along different timescales isn't just technically but also democratically necessary, all while disarmingly swirling a glass of port I'd nabbed off one of the main sponsor's tables (minesweeping is praxis, etcetera). Just as you should always know your audience, you should always know where to find the free fortified wine.

Beyond personal and party ideology, beyond electoral machinations, inattention and apathy, there are two obstacles to thinking about policy and planning in the long-term at the (somewhat ironically named) "constitutional" level in UK politics (ironic because the UK's lack of a single, written constitution is often cited as the source of many of its problems).

One of these challenges is the default stance of Treasury, which is deeply hostile to any policies which involve upfront investment for a long-term return. As one ex-mandarin put it, "I was trained to be sceptical of spend-now-save-later proposals," which I would suggest is a preposterous position for the government department singularly responsible for authorising revenue expenditure and distributing capital expenditure for an entire country.

The other challenge for the UK, both for long-term policymaking and for the devolution of power away from Westminster, is the nebulous and opaque concept of parliamentary sovereignty.

Parliamentary sovereignty can be summarised by three general rules: Parliament can create or end any law; the courts cannot overrule these laws; no Parliament can pass laws that a future Parliament cannot change.

With respect to long-term policymaking of the sort that's vital not just for planning and delivering transport infrastructure but also for other policy domains involving the managing and development of skilled workers (which is most of them), the interpretation of the last of these rules is a source of serious problems. It enables government to flip-flop on multi-billion-pound projects to such an extent that we have crippled our ability to deliver any significant infrastructure in the country whatsoever.

While not explicitly precluding the UK or its devolved authorities from setting long-term policy objectives *and sticking to them*, the combination of parliamentary sovereignty with Treasury's violent allergy to investing for the future creates a sort of governmental harmonic resonance which vibrates to the tips of every branch of the UK government.

There are more layers to this onion. Fiscal rules are the self-inflicted constraints on spending and taxation set by neoliberal governments at national, pan-national and international levels. In all cases they are functionally meaningless and exist as little more than a government's competence-signalling to financial and news institutions, comprising a great oversimplification of the value of the state and a mirror of the political consensus in which they were established.

Combine Treasury doctrine, parliamentary sovereignty, fiscal rules and the cross-party consensus — now well into its fifth decade — concerning the increasingly limited role of the elected state in creating and controlling the physical environment in which we live, and it is little wonder that we are so ill-equipped to apply known solutions to the challenges we face.

A line that frequently comes up in British politics is that one government should not "bind the hands" of any future government. This is little more than an excuse for inaction in any given policy domain, given government makes decisions that bind future administrations daily, but when it comes to policies that only see results after decades — such as the building of a new railway line or the training of a skilled pool of workers — then government is making active decisions that limit the opportunities for the future.

It's one thing to be suffering from a lack of forward planning in a country with a government that doesn't care, but the consequences for a future government that might care are currently plain to see in Germany.

The previous centre-right administration, led by the Christian Democratic Union (CDU) and incumbent for sixteen years, made little effort to invest in national rail infrastructure, preferring road expansion and championing the same perspectives at a European level.

Roll forwards to today: rapidly increasing demand is being accelerated by policy initiatives such as the immensely successful Deutschland-Ticket, allowing unlimited travel on (almost) all public transport for €49 per month. Yet the network cannot cope. A railway system that has always had a reputation for being unreliable, at least among Germans, was on its knees in 2022, with a third of trains running with significant delays and satisfaction with the quality of the system at a historic low.

In this case, rather than binding a future government by their action, the CDU have bound the hands of their successors by their *inaction*.

The value in my cornering the minister and pleading this case to him was pretty limited, not necessarily because he wasn't taking it in, not even because he wouldn't agree with small or large parts of it, but because the role of rail minister in the UK is an entirely ceremonial one, involving absolutely no power or responsibility. Barely a month later, in what amounted to little more than a job application to his next prospective employer, the UK prime minister, Rishi Sunak, cancelled High Speed 2 (leaving only the under-construction leg between outer London and Birmingham). In so doing, he shattered the last vestiges of any long-term plan for the UK railway and wider transport system.

Whether this decision is reversed by the next administration remains to be seen — I am not holding out hope — but its cancellation without any heed for the future somewhat confirms the viability of directionless transport policy.

Without the right incentives, decisions hostile to the future will be made over and over again.

# CHAPTER 2.3

# PUTTING POWER IN THE RIGHT PLACE

Our railways should be publicly owned. But this alone will not give us the network of railway networks we need to take on the future. Because if we do not also democratise those networks, they will not serve our needs. This means aligning the control structures of railway operations with the populations they serve — for example giving a city control over its suburban railway services. It also means ensuring adequate autonomy from central government to avoid short-term micro-management by departments and ministers.

And if we are to exploit the massive benefits of rail versus the alternatives — namely safety, efficiency and speed — we also need to create structures that integrate key interfaces rather than splitting them off into their own separate chunks. Having different companies owning the trains, running the trains, maintaining the trains and owning the tracks on which the trains run ensures that none of these organisations can benefit from the systemic efficiencies of, for example, lighter, cleaner and more-efficient electric trains or providing level boarding and independent, accessible travel.

Ownership, devolution, democratisation and integration: the recipe is simple. Let's understand how each ingredient is crucial to the result.

## Public versus private

Railways have always been tools of the prevailing political model of the day, and as a result have also been at the whim of it. In the world of the post-1970s economic consensus — the neoliberal consensus, if you like — fiscal and monetary policy have moved much of the world (but particularly the anglosphere) away from investing for the future and towards short-termist sticking plasters. The fear of the debt–GDP ratio has led countries like the UK to almost completely reject strategic planning, leaving the quality of its public services and the problems faced by its citizens to spiral out of control. This approach has only weakened economies and deepened debt crises globally. You can't dig your way out of a hole: at some point you have to buy a ladder.

Impotent fiscal and monetary orthodoxies — and the governments wedded to an outdated economic model that still deploys them — control the destinies of most people outside of India and China. This leaves a very narrow and ill-suited investment framework within which to solve the challenges we're talking about. Big problems require big solutions, and most governments are unwilling to pay for them. The idea that the private sector has the competence, confidence and — most pertinently — the cash to even begin to tackle these challenges at the scale required is laughable.

It's the biggest question that gets asked these days, and I have to say it is one of the least interesting to me: Should railways be nationalised? The answer, by the way, is a resounding "absolutely yes, railways should be in public hands and operated by one or more state entities, devolved appropriately," but as I said earlier, it's the first small step in a much larger journey, and so much more has to be gotten right than just shifting the ownership over from private to public.

It is, however, worth looking at how I can so quickly and hand-wavingly come to my answer. Let's start by using a simple rule that I like to apply to this question for any sizeable entity. It's the "Can it go bust?" rule.

If — indeed when — a Class 1 railroad or a national infrastructure operator goes bankrupt or into administration, does government let it fall over and allow the market to respond freely? No, they absolutely do not. When COVID-19 meant existing revenue models just broke, did governments let the private operators of public transport collapse? No, they backed them up with significant grant funding.

The British railway has shown that a franchised railway system of private operators will ultimately self-destruct. The response from reformers today is that a concession model (whereby a private company just comes in and runs the system specified for them by the local or national authority) is the solution, to which my reply is: What value is the private company adding at this point? It may keep a lot of lawyers and middle managers in work, but I don't see how this helps us to save costs, other than the traditional "private companies can squeeze the unions" argument.

(Incidentally, the "Can it go bust?" rule works for everything. Water and electricity companies? If they fail the test, they should be state owned. Banks? Nope. Outsourcing agencies? No. Big tech companies? Decidedly not. Companies that make those little plastic bug things on a spring that pop up after a seemingly random duration? Yeah, those can go bust and can stay private. You get the picture.)

If we return to our Top Twenty list of railway systems, twelve are essentially fully state owned, and all but five are running systems with significant state involvement and ownership. Contrary to the picture painted by the advocates of liberalised or private railway operation, it is private, highly liberalised railways that are the outliers.

Indeed, the five systems at the top of our Top Twenty list are all significantly (Austria, Switzerland) or entirely (China, India, Russia) state owned. Of the Top Twenty, only two are operated fully privately: Japan and the United States. We've already covered the mess that the US railroad system is in. It's doomed to collapse without significant if not wholesale nationalisation.

Meanwhile, Japan's privatised railway system is uniquely integrated, empowered as a property developer and configured almost entirely around high-density — and thus highly profitable — passenger railway operations. It is a unique arrangement, and it has not prepared Japan well for demographic or climate shifts. The lack of balance means that Japan relies heavily on road transport for its freight haulage. As its rural services become less viable under a private model, it is likely Japan will have to pursue significant reform.

Nevertheless, Japan's railway system shows that ownership is only one facet of the issue. A history of network expansion, a current government broadly supportive of further investment, and the integration of track and train combined with the split into autonomous, regionally aligned companies enables Japan's railway to operate highly effectively.

Conversely, those railway networks we described as merely "delivering" — those with middling success such as France, Germany or Finland — are all either entirely or majority state owned, and this hasn't stopped them from seeing service quality hit by strikes and a lack of long-term investment.

Indeed, Great Britain's railway system (remember, the Northern Irish system has remained fully nationalised) has been slowly returned back to public ownership as its various fragments have failed. The tracks are fully state owned, many of its train-operating companies are under the control of a state holding company, and much of the functions of the railway are directly contained within the Department for Transport — without any sort of coordination or purpose, continuing to bring more parts of the railway under state control as they fail will not result in a successful system. Nationalisation alone is not enough to give us the transport backbone we need.

Whether publicly or privately owned, an over-centralised national railway organisation will not deliver for the regions or cities across a country. A nationalised railway body run without sufficient autonomy from departmental or ministerial meddling will solve few of the problems major railways face. And a state-owned railway is not going to successfully harness the dominant energy efficiency of rail if the operators of track and train do not benefit from optimisation of each other's interconnected interfaces and technologies. The railway is a system, and it needs to be operated as such.

It is critical to balance democratisation, devolution and integration of a national railway system to deliver the maximum possible benefits.

## Devolution and democratisation

By the end of this decade, nearly a third of the world's population will live in cities of more than one million people. Cities of this size merit more than just a suburban passenger service running among other types of rail operation, and they require more capacity than a tram system alone can deliver — dedicated metro systems should be a key component of any urban population of this scale.

Meanwhile, 80% of the world's population will live in cities of all sizes by the middle of this century. This is no bad thing: cities are by far the most environmentally friendly way for humans to live. People don't have to travel far to reach all of the amenities they need, and the delivery of public services is generally much more efficient with high-population densities, not least public transport.

Accordingly, the most significant priority for rail transportation must be to provide high-capacity mass-transit capability in cities and their built-up surroundings, integrated with other public transport modes and scaled to match the desire of people to move along any given corridor.

Consequently, the control and oversight of urban rail systems must be aligned with a city's devolved authority. Devolution of funding and policymaking to suitably empowered city region authorities is key to allowing decision-making to more closely reflect the needs of the people using the system, ensuring local buy-in and democratic oversight. In turn, this localised view of the future incentivises long-term consensus between people and their representatives, meaning infrastructure projects can be progressed more rapidly.

Naturally, such control affords the ability to integrate transport modes to provide a uniform transport system, and while authorities controlling transport alone can fulfil these functions under the oversight of national government, the real value is achieved by looking beyond the limits of transport. Thinking more widely about spatial planning, development, and even utilities such as waste management and power generation is the way to truly unlock the potential of a city. This can only be achieved by the devolution of power and funding from central government to a devolved city region authority with the ability to raise funds by its own means.

Devolution of this kind is not free from challenges, particularly in relation to railways, which are integrated both physically (sharing tracks with regional, freight or intercity services) and technically (in relation to national technical standards). In ideal circumstances, a city's railway infrastructure would be fully segregated from the regional or national networks, simplifying operational boundaries and consequent responsibility, as well as enabling increased capacities.

On the other hand, every country has a requirement for intercity and other long-distance services that breach administrative borders, whether internal or international. These require central coordination and planning.

The retention of (or at least access to) the right skilled people to plan, maintain, develop and enhance a railway system can be challenging at a city or even regional level. This is a good example of where a strong and well-funded national railway organisation adds value, as it can act as a conduit for training, in collaboration with professional bodies and institutions, as well as driving forward useful national-level programmes that can enhance devolved railway operations. A large body like Deutsche Bahn or British Rail can train and retain expertise at a scale that would not be either viable or efficient at a city level.

Another critical element for railway operations is to avoid the duplication of necessarily laborious processes, such as the development, certification and introduction of new trains. While customisation is valuable at a devolved level, the technical specifications must be standardised as much as possible, at as high a level as possible, to ensure that connected railway networks can accommodate each other's trains on each other's tracks. Even where there aren't physical connections, there are benefits for efficient delivery of trains and infrastructure when there isn't too much duplication of design processes, components, assemblies, certifications and so on.

So we see in some more detail that there is a balance to be struck between devolution and centralisation. We also see that there is some pattern in the split — accepting the need for major projects to be coordinated at a high level, control and funding of railway operations and strategy is most accountable when devolved closest to the people who use the system. Meanwhile, technical standards and complex processes are best maintained at as high a level as possible to maximise sharing of best practice and avoid duplicated effort.

This helpfully divides the stuff people have an interest in — and time to be interested in — from the stuff that they are generally happier for skilled and experienced people to oversee. I have a lot of personal interest in what train timetables look like and where new lines might be opened. I have less interest (okay, I'm lying seeing as you and I may be outliers here) in the nuts and bolts of wheel-profile compatibility and the here and there of the latest radio communication protocols.

Accordingly, by handing people greater control over their railways, they will have greater personal ownership over the system and will be more inclined to use it. This democratisation, if done right, will also open up decision-making to people otherwise disenfranchised from electoral politics. Turnout in the UK for local and mayoral elections remains pretty dismal, and giving greater control over local transport networks will increase the relevance of these levels of government for people in cities and regions, particularly those that feel forgotten. As such, the restructuring and rebalancing of railway powers — including those over funding — can inject some adrenaline into our democracy.

## An integrated structure

The right industry structure is critical for innovation, too.

The links between academic and industrial research, testing, trials and full-scale validation and deployment were lost when British Rail's fantastic research division was broken up and privatised. Having given the world modern high-speed trains, solid-state signalling and more besides, subsequent and valiant efforts by the UK's railway research universities have struggled to find traction when it comes to full-scale testing and deployment. This derives directly from the lack of connection with industry, and with the fragmentation of that industry.

This leads us on to the lines along which any railway organisation may be sliced. We've already learned what the impact of fragmentation on national railway systems is, and there's a reason why, despite desperate efforts to break up national railway operators in mainland Europe, the mature markets have actually returned to unified railway organisations.

While there is clearly value in not just permitting but giving equal favour to operators crossing borders — particularly for the freight sector — this does not merit splitting the train and track operations of the incumbent state operators. Doing so removes some of the key incentives for long-term planning. A separate infrastructure operator has little or no incentive to expand their system or upgrade it with overhead electrification, which could be seen simply as adding to the list of its liabilities. Likewise, train operators will have little interest in facilitating a long closure of a line for major upgrades, as it will interrupt their operations and they will take the brunt of the public ire over trains not running.

## Fragmentation breeds chaos

Walk through the Great Hall at York's National Railway Museum to a set of doors next to the new café, and you'll have found the gates to a sanctuary of sorts. Within what is alternately called the open stores, the Warehouse or the North Shed is a treasure trove of railway paraphernalia so varied that it is almost pointless for me to even pick out a few highlights.

I'll just say that my favourite object among the tens of thousands on display here and indeed in the whole museum is what I refer to as Schrodinger's burger box, which is the packaging used to sell the "last" Great North Eastern Railway burger — someone was proud enough of to stick it in a glass box. It's sealed, so the next question is: Is the burger still in there? The museum has repeatedly ignored my calls for them to x-ray the thing.

I've spent hundreds of hours in here, and I literally always spot something new. No matter what your interest — even if you have no interest in railways at all — you'll find something in here that will fascinate you.

As you walk in and turn right, there's a tall rack on top of which rests a variety of surveying tools, and next to them is a sign saying "PRIZE LENGTH", which has its origin on a section of what was originally the unopposed Caledonian Railway main line between Perth and Aberdeen, before the North British Railway built their weavy route alongside it.

Lengths were the smallest breakdown of a railway company's infrastructure, usually running for no more than a few miles. Each length would have allocated to it a team of maintenance staff known as platelayers, usually consisting of a ganger and two or more trackmen. These gangs took great pride in their work, and upon the annual inspection by the chief engineer or chief inspector of the railway, they would be awarded the prize length for a particularly well-maintained and well-kept stretch of line.

In the case of our winning prize length sign, it was plonked next to the track somewhere between Stanley Junction near Perth and the county town of Forfar, signifying the win and encouraging the gang to fend off the competition the following year.

This was the frontline for delivering a functioning railway at the most granular level. At the other end of the management chain, things were not nearly as well organised, as government kept its distance from the melee of railway companies vying for routes and traffic (unlike MPs themselves, who regularly had personal financial interests in the railways they waved through Parliament).

As the tremendous boom in railway construction took hold of Britain, hundreds of railway companies built a hopeless tangle of lines, many duplicated, many more of very poor quality, all in an effort to unlock the maximum profit from this new frontier of capital. A not insignificant number of lines were entirely speculative, with their actual construction being an inconvenience to those profiting off the bubble.

Putting to one side the calamitous economic consequences when this bubble burst (which it did, in dramatic style, in 1847), the result was that Britain's railway network was and remains a complete mess. It bears little or no relationship to the administrative boundaries of Britain, which themselves make no sense either — an issue that is not unique to the UK. They also do not map well onto Britain's modern population distribution — direct rail links don't actually exist between many pairs of UK cities.

A good example is where our prize length from earlier came from: the former Scottish Midland Junction Railway, built in 1848 and later absorbed into the Caledonian

Railway, was of a far superior alignment to the North British Railway's parallel route that opened two decades later. Conversely, the Caledonian's route avoided most of the population centres along the East coast, whereas the North British line served most of them. Neither was, therefore, perfect, and the result is that today's main line linking to Aberdeen serves everywhere slowly and includes none of the Scottish Midland Junction Railway's original route. This is the picture across much of Britain. Private enterprise did not deliver us a good national railway.

If our platelaying gangs represented the dedicated, tactical side of railway delivery, then the strategic end of railway operations could be described as "corporate disarray" given the constant vying for shareholder profit and monopoly at the expense of goods customers and passengers alike.

What might it look like, though, if there were no localisation, engineering knowledge was scattered to the four winds, and rather than incentives for safety or quality, infrastructure was run as property investment and overseen by a contract management organisation?

At around midday on 17 October 2000, the UK would find out. As an InterCity 225 set heading northwards passed along a shallow but high-speed curve approaching Hatfield station, a thirty-five-metre length of rail shattered like a dropped vase under the left-hand wheels of the train.

Travelling at 115 mph, all but the front two vehicles derailed, and thanks to the lateral acceleration through the fast curve, the unrestrained vehicles scattered outwards, with the restaurant coach overturning and striking an overhead electrification mast. Four passengers in this vehicle died, and over seventy others were injured.

As crash investigators wandered back along the site to the point of the wreckage, around 1 km south of the derailed train, they identified two things that alarmed them.

The first was the shattered rail, which had completely disintegrated under traffic. Rails are not flimsy little paperclips — each metre weighs over fifty kilograms — so the condition this rail had been allowed to reach under traffic was clearly well beyond acceptable. The second cause for alarm was a third, loose rail set in the fourfoot between the running rails, left in place to be installed as a replacement.

As it happens, both observations were key to understanding the cause of the accident. The first led to significant research into the behaviour of railway rails under severe stresses, and the consequent improved understanding of rolling contact fatigue changed the design and maintenance of railways in the UK and beyond. I still refer back to this accident in my day job as a design engineer and when teaching.

The second is more pertinent to our discussion. It was the smoking gun that uncovered a litany of failures in the organisation and a lack of empowerment (or employment) of the people with the right skills.

Railtrack had been formed as part of the atomisation of British Rail in the mid-1990s, and it had been created primarily as a contract management organisation, retaining as little of its specialist engineering knowledge as possible by design. The structure of the industry around it involved multiple separate contractors, subcontractors and sub-subcontractors. Consequently, skills and knowledge were split apart in such a way that no single responsible person was both competent and empowered enough to match engineering knowledge to decision-making. Those high enough up the tree to attempt to flag the problem faced intransigence (at best) from upper management in Railtrack.

Railtrack itself had an incentive structure shaped not around prioritising safety but around minimising train delays at all costs. It did not create sufficient space in the railway timetable to allow inspections in accordance with its own standards.

The outsourced maintenance contractor did not comply with engineering standards in relation to defect management or carry out inspections to the level of detail required. They did not employ staff competent to inspect or assess track defects or the maintenance techniques employed to minimise the risks resulting from them. Grinding trains that could prolong rail life were operated by a separate contractor, and infrequently. Guidelines as to the use of grinding were held by Railtrack's central engineering team. Ultrasonic testing was screaming on each pass that the rail was essentially shagged, but this received little attention from the maintenance contractor.

Records were sent to Railtrack's zonal management, but few staff at this level were capable of reviewing them. The view of its highly paid executive staff was that Railtrack was a contracts manager and not an engineering organisation. This led to contempt for engineering skills and the recruitment of totally unqualified staff, among whom there was also high turnover. The zone-compliance and engineering manager responsible for the section of track around Hatfield failed to comprehend what track work was being undertaken and what was required "because of its technical nature". The zone quality standards manager, in his own words, "did not have the knowledge of railway engineering nor railway safety".

In the words of the independent investigation published nearly six years later, "Railtrack was not putting safety as the number one objective in its maintenance strategy."

Today, there are no prize lengths and there are no length gangs. Thankfully Britain has dispensed with Railtrack (though not until after another dramatic and fatal derailment with similar root causes), and its infrastructure is now managed by state-owned Network Rail. Maintenance is undertaken in-house, but recent political machinations are threatening this. For now, though, there are still teams who have a local knowledge of the railway they look after.

## Bigger problems

The UK has its own unique problems when it comes to over-centralisation, but every country faces challenges in the way power is distributed. For the UK, power needs to be wrestled away from Treasury prior to its abolishment and splitting into multiple departments with a more future-facing remit based around opportunity and wellbeing.

Ultimately, facilitating the creation of the right railway structure requires these bigger challenges to be tackled too — the railways do not exist in a vacuum. And this requires greater democratic involvement at all levels. This should be seen as positive, even if it's a bit circular — to resolve the democratic challenges we collectively face requires more democratic involvement and participation in those systems that we've seen fail time and time again.

The framework of accountability I've outlined, and the organisational structures and lines of command it creates, must be robust enough to allocate the right responsibilities at the right levels. It must understand the required skills and respond accordingly. Because skills remain the most critical resource on and off the railway, and without a plan to make the best use of skilled people, we will not be able to deliver the railway the future needs us to. As things are, we are falling short.

# CHAPTER 2.4

# WITHOUT A PLAN, WE'RE DOOMED

After setting the mission and creating the structure of the rail industry, the most important tool with which to direct its efforts is the long-term plan.

When I talk about long term, I don't mean ten years ahead. I don't even mean twenty years ahead. Modern railway infrastructure can be built to have a design life of 120 years, and I see no reason not to be planning for a railway network for the end of this century.

In any case, a long-term plan should look to capture the end-state of the network as best as we can currently assess it. The timeline for the delivery of that plan can come later, but we should build the future we want to live in, and that starts with painting a picture of what it looks like.

The benefits of such a plan are extremely far-reaching. Industry and its supply chains can prepare for delivering projects by developing the right sort of skills and capabilities. The workforce can be sustainably grown and developed. Reliance on insecure contract staff can be reduced, ideally to zero, which improves staff safety and wellbeing. Rolling programmes of infrastructure improvement can be undertaken, rather than isolated and inefficient projects. Lessons can be learnt and exploited — not forgotten because there's a five- or ten-year gap between similar schemes. Service planners can more effectively shape timetables, forecast usage and predict the need for change over a longer timescale. All of this unleashes a better use of resources, including operational and capital expenditure.

The other benefit of such a plan is that the public can comment on it, be involved in its development and understand when their local services will see improvements (and what these will look like). Openness and transparency are great ways of engaging and uniting people both within and outside of the rail industry.

A plan also allows the public to hold politicians accountable. We are already seeing this with the Climate Change Committee's reporting on governments' progress on delivering the net-zero obligations of the 2008 Climate Change Act.

One of the things that most aggravates politicians about railways is that there's almost nothing you can announce in a press release that will have meaningful consequences within an election cycle. Having a plan helps with this, as governments can lay claim to increased progress in delivering the plan. They get to create press releases relating to railway projects without having to wait several decades for a final outcome.

While it isn't actually that different from the normal way economies are projected into the future, I think a useful way of reframing the issue is to think about what we are handing to our children. What legacy are we leaving behind? If politicians thought more about the legacy they'll leave behind once they're dead, rather than about what happens while they are still in office, then we might see a shift in their time horizon.

Policymaking is only useful when considered alongside its temporal and spatial dimensions. That's a fancy way of saying that the time it takes to implement a policy and see a result and the geographical reach of that policy should influence how and where that policy is put in place and the extent to which it can be meddled with.

Similarly, these policies have relationships across domains. The way in which people and goods are moved is closely related to a given country's broader industrial and business policies. There is a direct relationship with education and training policy given the need for skilled people to develop, design and deliver railway services, at all levels. Energy policy and transport are closely related, not least as railways need cheap energy to operate, ideally in the form of nuclear or renewably generated electricity. Trade and commerce rely on the uninterruptible flow of goods more than ever before, as supply chains have become more streamlined and less resilient, and this clearly relates directly to transport policy too.

What we are describing is a huge, tangled web of causal links, with hundreds of inputs and outcomes. When you muck around with one, it makes all of the others jiggle and wiggle about to a greater or lesser extent, and it can be very difficult to predict exactly how.

For any time-limited government, even one with the best of intentions, managing these complexities alongside the temporal and spatial realities of each policy domain requires plans that can be compared with each other. And few policy domains cut across all others as much as transport.

Fundamentally, to take the railway of today and shape it into the railway of the future requires us to plan out what that railway needs to look like.

## Creating the plan

The first thing that is needed in order to create a national plan for rail is to develop the ideal service specification across all public transport types that delivers the modal shift required not just for today's total mobility, but accounting for the increased mobility resulting from demographic shifts, increased accessibility and wider prosperity.

This service specification should not start at the national level, though. The devolved authorities will both know and should be held accountable to deliver the services needed by passengers and industry, and so it should be the minimum service specifications developed at a city and regional level that then feed up into the national plan. Once overlaid with the national services, such as intercity and strategic freight, the appropriate transport modes can be associated with each service.

At this point you have a virtual transport system linking all of the nodes of a theoretical network. Each theoretical connector will have a minimum capacity required to deliver the national service specification. For now, though, the theoretical network will bear little resemblance to the real world.

It is when this theoretical network is overlaid onto the existing, real network that it becomes possible to see where the proposed future service specification can be delivered using existing (if modified) lines, or where new lines are required.

The difference between the current network and this end-state network gives the picture of where change needs to occur and where enhancement work needs to take place.

## Growing a network from first principles

Let's look more closely at how the theoretical service specification — a sort of perfect timetable, if you will — can be developed.

This isn't going to be a lesson in timetable creation. Frankly, creating transport timetables is a dark and underappreciated art that I'm ill-equipped to pontificate about in any great detail. However, policymakers and politicians often apply certain pre-conditions or restrictions on the process of modelling transport services, and I want to pick through a few of these to highlight how today's practice and tomorrow's needs are too often severely disconnected.

We've selected a mode-share target as our single driving objective.

Say our legislation gets passed, the mode-share target passes into law and the UK suddenly has a binding mission for its railways to achieve by a set date. Doing so would naturally necessitate consideration of all transport modes, not just rail, which in turn would require the input of all levels of government: not just Westminster, but the devolved nations, city regions and councils.

Mode share describes the means of flow of people and goods. These flows are complex, with tidal flows like those in travel to work areas, and linear flows along major corridors. Transport flow is fractal, with urban sprawl (residential or otherwise) acting like small branches, feeding larger branches, feeding into trunks, which then split out into branches again in urban areas. Different means of travel overlay onto each other, perhaps with slightly different trunks (such as a motorway, railway, metro line, heavily used bus route, etc.), but all will map together to show broad flows of people between and within urban areas.

The UK has a reasonably detailed model of what is known as origin-destination (OD) data, derived from survey and census and available in secure form at a detailed level and more openly at a higher level. This data provides a very clear picture of the types of journeys people undertake, and how they undertake them. Indeed, this data is what informs the current mode-share figures.

As an example, let's stick to the city I live in, and make use of the most recent census travel data. This data was for during the pandemic, so numbers will be lower than normal, but they still paint a useful picture.

There were around two thousand people living in York and travelling to work in Leeds at the last census. Commuters choosing to drive will very likely have taken the A64 for most of the route. Those riding the train will almost all have been on the main line shared by local and cross-country services passing through Church Fenton and Cross Gates. Thus the main trunk route here is provided by these two pieces of infrastructure, on which we can account for two thousand different journeys and the consequent mode share.

We can repeat this for other routes too. Sticking with the flow of workers in and out of Leeds, the largest flow of all was from Bradford and its surrounding environs, accounting for over seventeen thousand people. Those in the car will have chosen to use either the A647 via Pudsey or drive down onto the M62 and use the M621 to get into Leeds. Those on the train have two choices as well, with direct diesel trains from Bradford Interchange, or the slightly less direct electric services from Bradford Forster Square via Shipley. The trunks may be bifurcated, but they are still trunks.

Given railways are best suited to these trunk flows, these are the numbers that allow us to understand what the capability of the railway system needs to be. If the railway is targeting a mode share of 25% passenger flow, then between York and Leeds it needs to carry at least enough capacity to accommodate five hundred passengers in morning and evening commuting periods. Both railways between Bradford and Leeds need to accommodate a total of at least four thousand passengers over the course of the commuting peak.

Of course, the trunks don't just carry one OD flow. They carry many flows, including people travelling from further afield or those travelling for other reasons, as well as goods traffic using the same route. Travellers from Hull, Newcastle or further afield, and those travelling to Sheffield, Manchester or beyond will all also be using the same corridor as our five hundred York-to-Leeds passengers. Once you overlay the national OD data, the total figures reveal themselves.

Any consideration of future flows must be aspirational, accounting for an increase in total flows as well as just that from a greater modal share. Relying exclusively on the latest OD data means embedding travel patterns that exist today and recreating existing patterns of inequality and access to work. We'll talk about who the railways should be for in Chapter 2.7 (spoiler alert: everyone), but if rail is adapted to be accessible to all, then more people will travel who aren't captured in the existing OD data. If more people are brought within reach of rail through improved public transport, better-connected housing, better childcare provision, higher minimum wages (and thus fewer hours needing to be worked) and so on, then once again the OD data alone is inadequate.

Thus, proposed trunk capacity should not just be an increase on the percentage of the current overall flow between sets of origins and destinations, but should take account existing *and future* total populations between and beyond those points, considering what total level of mobility might be achieved if societal inequality was reduced and more of the population had access to the resources (money *and* time) that made greater travel for work and leisure an option.

This isn't a particularly left-leaning point — anyone almost anywhere on the political spectrum should want more people to have more access to more work and leisure options, because this means more opportunities, better matches between people and roles, higher productivity and more money being spent.

Of course, to achieve a mode-share target for rail requires punitive policy measures to disincentivise driving. In the UK's case, the need to shift towards a system of road pricing as the use of electric vehicles picks up presents a powerful lever to support rail's targets. City authorities should also have greatly expanded powers over their road networks, allowing them to direct policy towards favouring sustainable modes in accordance with the needs of their communities and spatial plans.

This is also true for goods and industry — organising smaller businesses together can allow their collective loads to be carried on rail alongside larger shippers.

Let's focus for the time being on what this means for the resources and workers required, and how we can plan to deliver them and in turn achieve our mode-share targets.

Stepping back and looking at "the journey" in abstract gives us more insights that are invaluable for modelling how a railway system (and the wider transport system) should look. Any journey involves branches at each end and a trunk in the middle — in other words, there are phases of the journey where the number of users sharing that particular part of the journey is lower, and phases of the journey where the number is higher. The number of users sharing the part of your journey from your front door to the street is very low. The number of people sharing your trip down your street is a little higher. As you continue your trip, the volume of fellow users will generally rise then fall as you split off the trunk again as you near your destination.

A traditional view of travel looks generally only at one end of this trip and considers the other end to be the arrival at a built-up area (like bankers arriving from the London suburbs into the City, at which point they all work within a short distance of each other anyway). However, travel is more diverse than this. It may be that a journey actually involves stringing multiple trunks together, or it may avoid trunks altogether.

So we've talked roughly about how both nodes and connectors can give us figures for how many people we should be accommodating on our railway. But to what extent can we consider these people as a homogenous group who will all sit on any train that we provide them? Well, this depends on what sort of journey they are making. Longer-distance travellers value speed more than frequency; for shorter-distance travellers, the opposite is generally true. In the UK, there has been shown to be an S-curve that defines passenger behaviour in relation to the choice between rail and air. To reach 50% market share versus aviation, rail journeys need to be four hours or shorter. Usefully, this covers most long-distance travel in the UK. Drop journey times to three hours, and market share rises to 80% or more.

This broadly applies elsewhere, though the figures change depending on other factors such as the quality of connecting transport both to the airports and competing intercity railway route. Generally, though, high-speed rail that runs parallel to air routes can reduce aviation demand by between 20% and 80% if journey times and connections are well optimised.

What is referred to by transport planners as "generalised journey time" usually accommodates both requirements, which is useful, as the majority of passenger kilometres travelled are on longer journeys where travellers are thinking about both frequencies and speeds. They want the branch element of the journey to be served by a high-frequency mode so they can focus on planning around the trunk element, and they want the trunk element to be quick so that their overall journey is as short and pain-free as possible, freeing up more time in the day for them to do other things.

Consequently, mode share also gives us a feel for the specification of our system. Do we prioritise speed, frequency, or a balance of the two?

On some transport corridors, only one type of rail service is necessary. In undeveloped areas between cities, long-distance high-speed services minimise both journey times and the number of trains needed to shift large numbers of people. Once you reach the urban sprawl, however, the demands on the railway can become more complex. Long-distance trains generally and correctly just serve the major urban centre, while suburban services provide links across the wider built-up area.

The highest-capacity railway is a railway where all of the trains do the same thing, one after the other, meaning they can move like a conveyor belt in unison, delivering the maximum passenger (or freight) throughput on the infrastructure. A simple two-track railway can deliver massive capacity when only used by one service pattern like this.

Conversely, a railway that mixes two or more service types will always compromise total passenger throughput. In the example of our train from York to Leeds, the long-distance services might be passing southwards from Scotland or Newcastle on their way towards the Midlands and Bristol. Regional services may be traversing their way from Scarborough to Manchester. Local services will be calling at places like Church Fenton, Garforth and Cross Gates. Freight services might be passing through on their way to quarries in the Pennines.

We have the tools today to model all of this complexity. It is a situation where iterative modelling — machine learning, for example — can develop idealised networks that optimise the arrangement of nodes, connectors and required capacity. But if we are to succeed in creating a plan based on widespread consensus, this process cannot be undertaken without people having a direct say over what they think their future should look like.

## Consult early, consult well

Any major proposals that result in impacts to the built and natural environment tend to meet opposition. In some countries, this opposition is swept aside without any hesitation. In other countries, vehement opposition to projects results in their being curtailed or cancelled, or in their never getting off the drawing board in the first place.

Empowering people to have a say over what gets built through their land is crucial — particularly in places with indigenous or economically deprived populations. There are too many examples of transport projects, including railways, either misleading or ignoring local populations in their planning and construction.

In southern Mexico, the 1,000-mile long Tren Maya project has been a classic case study in the worst of civil engineering indifference. Consent was sought from the local populations along the route without providing them the information needed to properly assess the threat the line posed them. The line has now destroyed countless unique limestone cave systems as well as needlessly flattening vast tracts of rainforest as a result of inadequate design requiring late changes to the route.

However, even if we assume that the right structures of government have been established, such projects will still see opposition. If the process of involving and empowering neighbouring populations is not properly managed, this opposition will threaten humanity's ability to deliver the railway systems it needs.

To see this off at the head, consultation needs to start at the proposal stage, not the planning stage. When people are involved in decisions about the services they will get, they will be much more likely to understand and support the physical changes to their environment required to deliver them. If someone has, alongside their neighbours, agreed or even campaigned for an improved railway service, it is harder for them to turn around and say no when they are presented with the options for new infrastructure that will deliver them.

As well as requiring great strides in devolving power away from central government (at least for the UK), this requires a far more strategic view of consultations and planning. Unfortunately, strategy is often lacking for railway planning, partly because of political appetite, but often also because they are immensely complex systems that require decades of foresight. So too does society at large, and it is clear to me that thinking on a far longer-term basis about planning is how we can tackle bigger problems beyond railways too.

Today, planning and early consultations very quickly get mired in business cases, benefit-cost ratios and bundles of figures that lose the interest of even the most ardent of wonks, let alone the politicians and campaigners. This isn't right. Few have time to sift through a thousand-page report, and as a result, people don't get a chance to get involved.

How better to make this point than with a brief look back at why HS2 — Britain's only attempt at proper long-term planning in any domain for at least half a century — has failed?

To this day, and despite most of it being consigned to the scrap heap by a dying political party, High Speed 2 still represents a vital step-change in capacity for Britain's railway network. By moving high-speed trains onto their own dedicated lines, a huge amount of space is freed for more high-density passenger services and, just as critically, more freight.

The problem throughout its development, however, has been that this story was not told. Even more painfully, with the UK's overcentralised system of government meaning that the only real decision-making about transport happens in Westminster, almost nothing was done to realise the potential of this step-change regionally, and certainly not publicly. These omissions were a deliberate choice to enable Treasury a pathway for withdrawal from the project, but they are also why HS2 failed — its cost had nothing to do with it.

To this day, well over a decade after the project was proposed, much of the population are rightly confused about what the new railway is for and what impact it will have on them. Those in the public eye who supported the line often made the wrong arguments in favour of it, and those who oppose it still don't remotely understand its purpose.

Those with the most knowledge about the project and what it could unlock had Downing Street breathing down their necks, and there was very little of value they could say that described wider benefits, such as those for local populations. For the most part, their communications strategists convinced themselves that keeping their heads down and fielding as few questions as possible was the best course of action. In doing so, they relinquished the microphone to the project's critics, who could spout any old rubbish unchallenged.

The lack of any viable positive narrative meant that, from the perspective of the flailing Conservative Party in government, there were no political downsides to cancelling increasingly large parts of it.

Even with a supportive government in power, how do politicians justify spending what, for most of the public, appears to be a very large sum of money on something the same public don't believe they'll benefit from and for which politicians cannot articulate any meaningful benefits in the first place?

The consequence of High Speed 2 not being part of a wider, total-transport strategy for the UK is that it was impossible to describe the future which it occupied, and therefore it was also impossible to explain how that future would benefit individuals. And now the project has been mostly sunk, potentially kicking the benefits of high-speed segregation another generation away.

We have seen this story play out again and again with other types of rail enhancement. Investment in Britain's railways can be optimistically described as "stop-start". Without being part of a bigger picture, such investments are entirely at the whim of electoral bargaining.

Delaying investment only costs more money, given the inevitability of the work in question, and the carbon cost of delaying modal shift is catastrophic. The lack of a long-term strategic vision of what the railway should look like is not just highly wasteful; it is actively harmful.

This is no less true in the case of planning for a future where the segregation of long-distance, high-speed services means that the existing network must function very differently.

## Keeping things simple

High Speed 2 was intended to overcome a challenge for most of the railways of the world: How do you meet the complex needs of a national railway system, and all the diversity of travel and logistical requirements that entails, when mixing traffic means making less-optimised use of valuable and expensive infrastructure?

On any national corridor, there will be a mixture of local, regional and long-distance travellers. The needs of these travellers can be instructive as to what service needs to be provided for them. This is where the value of segregating different types of railway service onto their own systems comes into its own — being able to consider long-distance passengers broadly in isolation from the local and commuter services is very useful from the perspective of timetable-planning, infrastructure specification and devolution.

Planning a timetable where multiple services are running on the same lines is clearly more complicated than planning a timetable where services keep to their own tracks. The physical and operational needs of a mixed-traffic railway are much more complex than for a railway running one type of service. If you have a city region that wishes to own and operate its suburban rail services, it is much easier to facilitate and coordinate this when those services run on their own tracks, rather than sharing them with regional or long distance services.

In Britain, where two-track railways carry suburban, regional, long-distance and freight services, there is little more that can be squeezed from the network as it stands. This was what High Speed 2 was all about, and indeed should be what all long-distance high-speed infrastructure aims to unlock: a simplification and densification of services running on the existing railway, if indeed there is a paralleling railway.

Ultimately, there are two options available for service segregation. One option is the construction of new urban lines used only by urban services, and the other is the construction of new high-speed lines used by long-distance services. Both have merit, but the benefit of high-speed lines is that the existing network is often already running through built-up areas with stations (or former stations) that can have their services boosted once the trains that would otherwise pass without stopping shift onto the high-speed line.

It's possible not to segregate services. The Swiss and Austrians have done this with reasonable success, though they do not have particularly long distances to travel within their borders. Indeed, many of the long-distance routes, both old and new, that cut their way through and under the Alps mix all traffic types on the same two tracks.

This also steers us towards the specification of the system — overhead electrification is a must, and all trains must be electric to ensure the maximum acceleration and closest performance to fit as many trains onto the tracks as possible. Signalling must be particularly robust. And maintenance costs are high as annual tonnages will be enormous.

Even so, such an arrangement necessarily sacrifices either local frequency or long-distance journey times. Investment levels for such a railway must also be enormous. The UK has achieved this on much of the network, running one of the highest-density railways in the world, and the system is extremely costly to operate as a result.

Investments in mixed-traffic main lines are a case of diminished returns as a result, too. The West Coast Main Line, linking London, Birmingham, Liverpool, Manchester and on to Glasgow, is one of the busiest mixed-traffic railways in Europe. The original lines were built by George and Robert Stephenson as the backbone of Britain's intercity network, and it still retains this role today. There is no better recent example of the challenges in maximising throughput than the West Coast route modernisation (WCRM), which delivered far short of its promised outcomes at far greater cost than originally envisaged. Its failure as a project is what led directly to the development of High Speed 2, though the UK has managed to forget all this and cancel HS2 again barely a decade on from WCRM's failure.

This is true of the types of operators running on a railway as well. Today, private open-access operators run alongside the largely state-administered services running on the other side of the UK, up and down the East Coast Main Line. These services are both pitched and perceived as providing benefits to passengers through competition. On a railway network as saturated and under-capacity as the British rail network, this is fiction.

The open-access operators are in fact entirely extractive. They rely on an existing pool of trained staff and maintenance facilities, and on tracks that would not exist without incumbent operators and services. They block train paths that could and should be used by the integrated operator, add complexity for travellers, and most insidiously, act as a severe obstacle for optimisation of timetables as they have their own, fixed patterns of service that cannot be tweaked and adjusted as part of the wider whole. They are a false economy, draining revenue with no real benefits for passengers at all. The idea that there can be meaningful competition on the railways as a geographic monopoly is bizarre, and railways should not be competing with each other in any case — it is with road and air that the real competition lies.

## Waste and capacity

Specifying a system or service is easiest when it is shaped to deliver as simple a strategic objective as possible — in our case, a modal share value for public transport. The single key variable can then drive decisions about volumes of service, which in turn can provide numbers for staffing, assets and other resources.

Deploying these services, then, is best done by keeping the system as simple as possible. Duplication is perfectly acceptable if it enables maximised and efficient delivery as well as more accountability over those services.

Duplication is often described as waste when it comes to public services, and it shouldn't be. Coming off the back of a global pandemic, we've learned a lot about the relationship between capacity and waste.

For the purposes of this book, it is useful to think about waste as being Good and Bad.

Good Waste is the consequence of providing adequate capacity for peaks in demand, for example using trains that are long enough to accommodate peak passenger demand, but which are therefore less occupied for services outside of those peaks.

Bad Waste results from unnecessary duplication or complexity, such as when you outsource the upkeep of your buildings to a third party instead of directly employing those staff internally, resulting in significant expenditure on commercial and legal staff to maintain the invisible boundaries between organisations working under the same roof.

The two intercity railways I travel most on are Britain's East Coast Main Line, running up from London Kings Cross to York and beyond, and the Cross Country route, running up from the West Country through the Midlands and into Yorkshire and the North East. Both lines merge in York before heading northwards towards Scotland.

Much like the West Coast Main Line, both lines are complex, mixed use railways. The East Coast Main Line is essentially full, with every possible train path used and long-distance trains built as long as they can, given track, station and signalling limitations. The Cross Country Route is a mish-mash of various other main line railways, and for various reasonably stupid reasons the long-distance trains are far from being as long as they can be. Trains are in most cases half the length that they could be, meaning passengers on the busiest sections of the route are often playing a game of sardines in cramped, ageing trains. Unlike the East Coast Main Line, which starts and ends in capital cities, the Cross Country route links several of Britain's major cities but runs into less-populated regions at its extremities. One of the arguments for trains being so much shorter than their maximum possible length is that the lower populations at the limits of the route mean train loadings (how many passengers they carry) are significantly lower on these fringes, undermining the business case for longer trains.

This is incentivised by Britain's train leasing model, whereby the cost for train operators to lease a train does not reflect the cost of actually owning and running the train. It does not cost twice as much to run twice the length of train — staffing, maintenance and other costs per coach diminish as train length increases. Nevertheless, my experiences on the East Coast Main Line, with its system capacity essentially reached, is generally that you can find a seat. I travel regularly to London and back at all times of the day and rarely have to stand, even if trains are very busy. Meanwhile, on the Cross Country route, I'm often on the morning train from York towards Derby or Birmingham, and it's almost unheard of for me to get a seat unless I find a spot on a luggage rack.

Here, then, is an example of where waste provides a significant benefit to staff and passengers alike. Running longer trains that might be largely empty at the fringes of the service would greatly release the bottleneck on capacity in the high-demand core of the route.

You can see how this logic applies to other domains. The National Health Service (NHS) is one of the greatest things the UK has created and certainly one of few things we can really be proud of on the international stage. It is far from perfect, but one complaint I hear a lot is that it would run a lot better "if we could only get rid of the waste".

The NHS is still highly ranked when compared to other systems around the world. Given the NHS is the fifth-largest employer in the world and has an estate spread across the country of thousands of properties, containing millions of tools and machines and processing billions of medicines a year, it isn't just reasonable that there is some percentage of waste — it is desirable. What impact on services would result from eradicating this waste? What additional administrative costs would be incurred? What extra harm from a lack of availability of resources?

The NHS is inarguably struggling not from an excess of waste, but from a lack of it. Because waste is really just a side effect of adequate capacity, and we've seen how important adequate health system capacity is in our response to COVID-19.

Back to railways.

One of the most challenging elements in introducing new trains on a route is driver training. How do you train your drivers on the new trains when they are all rostered to drive the old trains on timetabled services? It is a problem usually solved with overtime, utilising a bit of goodwill and some extra pay to create the overlap in driver availability to transfer crews from one type of train onto the other.

However, it's finely balanced. Delays in the arrival of the new trains, problems with existing trains or infrastructure, coincident changes in timetable and fleet or — hypothetically — the complete breakdown in goodwill of staff towards their employers thanks to large-scale erosions in pay and conditions… these all contribute to making a railway service fall over right at the point when new trains are supposed to enhance it.

Decades of thinning driver numbers to the barest minimum and relying on overtime not just to manage foreseeable peaks in required hours but simply to maintain business as usual is a recipe for calamity, undermining the reliability of the service, reducing ridership and revenue and driving people back into their cars or into the skies. It isn't worth it.

It feels fairly clear that, in developing our strategic plan, we need to ensure that we account for the value of retaining — or indeed, creating — duplication, of capacity, and also not be afraid of waste.

## Projects versus programmes

Very few types of upgrade work are better delivered as discrete projects than as programmes of ongoing work.

The railway needs to move away from the use of business cases for determining the need for expansion, and instead rely on a long-term picture of the future. Doing so would allow the industry and its enormous and complex supply chain to cluster common or similar types of work together to maximise efficiency. That means less time, less money, fewer machines and fewer people — freeing them up to deliver more work elsewhere, and allowing the overall plan to be completed sooner. When it comes to reducing greenhouse gas emissions, as well as unlocking all the other benefits we've talked about, time really is of the essence.

This is reasonably well understood — and in most countries applied — in the building of overhead electrification, renewing of tracks, refurbishing of trains, making stations more accessible and so on. But the logic of a programme- rather than a project-led delivery plan applies to almost all other forms of work. Even massive and unique projects like major station construction or large-area resignalling projects can actually be delivered by teams that have worked on similar schemes. Here we see the benefits, too, of having significant engineering capability at the national core rather than fully devolving it out to the cities and regions, as the number of major national schemes can justify the retention of dedicated, well-adapted teams.

This is better for many other reasons beyond direct efficiency. With more confidence in the long-term pipeline of work, the supply chain can invest in processes, machines and staff. As well as being better paid, workers would get more confidence in their own roles and futures, improving their wellbeing and quality of life.

Eventually, the UK will have a high-speed network that will have a transformative impact on mobility and the economy, and to maximise these benefits, government needs to rearrange the existing network accordingly. This can only be achieved by the devolution of power away from the centre, but coordinating multiple regional and city authorities making changes to a fundamentally national network requires a plan.

In Part 1 we looked in detail at a number of national railway systems to see what we could learn about optimising rail operations. In Part 2, we've developed an incentive-based framework for planning a railway system from first principles.

In turn, this can provide us with an understanding of who we need in order to deliver the plan, how we can organise those people and how we ensure they are held accountable by the people who will use or benefit from the railway.

# CHAPTER 2.5

# MANY HANDS MAKE LIGHT WORK

The railways provide a solid link between our past and our future. Whether walking out along the railway with a pencil in hand to review its condition or undertaking localised maintenance by bashing it with a big steel rod, many of the roles that require people to put boots on ballast have remained the same since the inception of the railways many centuries ago. As technology and society have advanced around us, very few jobs still offer that link.

The reason I work in the rail industry — I design railways for a living, and it is literally my dream job — is because it feels like my calling, it makes a difference to the world, and is immensely gratifying as a result.

However, the reason I love working for the railways is that it is, more than anything else, an industry full of passionate people who care about running — or creating the space to run — better railway services. It is an industry of immense skill and care, and meeting and collaborating with those people fills me with excitement and delight.

Without these people, the railways would be nothing.

And yet, across the world, these people are taken for granted by the ultimate powers who control the railways. Whether it is the pressure applied to their working conditions or safety, to their ability to grow and retain skills, or to their ability to join the industry in the first place, workers on the railways are not given the opportunities they need to thrive, and consequently the railway cannot thrive either.

If we see the railway as a necessary — indeed critical — component in the way humanity tackles the challenges of the future, then in turn we need a plan to deploy them as quickly, fairly and effectively as possible.

That plan enables us to understand the shape of the railway, what assets and technologies it will need, how it will operate and who it will serve.

However, that plan cannot be delivered without skilled and dedicated people. Whether it is planners, engineers, drivers, signallers, managers, surveyors, cleaners, fitters — I honestly can't even capture a representative selection of the roles required to run a railway, the list is so diverse and all-encompassing — each individual requires skills that cannot be willed into existence by policy alone. To grow and retain the workforce needed to deliver the future, the most important thing is to develop that plan and stick to it. But a plan alone is not enough.

We need to empower organised labour through increased power and involvement of unions. We need to get rid of outdated silos and categories of skills types, not least jettisoning the "STEM" initialisation and many of its associated initiatives into the sun, to maximise the number and diversity of people joining the industry. Most of all, we need to totally reverse the atomisation and fragmentation of the rail industry, reintegrating much of the wider outsourcing supply chain into the national or devolved railway organisations.

Before we go into further detail on each of these points, though, it is necessary to understand the scale of the skills shortage, and some of the history behind its origins.

## The skills shortage

The blunt reality is that, today, we don't just face an uphill struggle in growing the workforce of the future — we are chronically short of people to deliver railway services today.

"The US Bureau of Labor Statistics projects a need for about 25,000 new civil engineers each year throughout this decade," explained Dennis D. Traux, president of the American Society of Civil Engineers, in late 2022.

A survey from January 2023 undertaken by Deutsche Industrie-und Haldelkammer (DIHK), Germany's chambers of commerce and industry, suggests that more than half of German companies found difficulty in employing the staff they needed, with technical and engineering firms reporting the most extreme pressures. The following month, another report by the European Investment Bank correlated slower-than-necessary growth in green technologies with a lack of skilled workers. There are similar challenges across Asia, with China reporting a shortage of as many as thirty million skilled workers.

In a globalised world, these pressures are not restricted by borders.

With economic need comes the risk, if not the inevitability, of exploitation of people crossing borders to work, despite their providing vital skills. This is an international problem — almost all countries are reporting shortages in skilled people, and climate change is only going to increase the demand for problem solvers globally. Shifting skilled people between borders isn't enough — the overall numbers need to increase.

We know skilled people across the board are in short supply as the world faces an unprecedented workforce shortage at all levels. But it isn't just recruitment that's driving shortages. Various surveys have shown that an increasing percentage of companies are finding retention of staff to be a key issue. The world isn't just struggling to recruit the staff that it needs — it is struggling to hold on to the staff it already has.

In the midst of this, we have a railway industry across the globe that is struggling to compete with other sectors. In some countries, particularly the UK and US, the rail industry is pressurising its staff with worsening pay and working conditions, increased responsibilities without the required additional training, and an inconsistent drip-feed of investment in trains and tracks, piling stress on staff as existing assets struggle to cope with demand.

The UK has inflicted significant pressure on its pool of skilled people following its departure from the European Union, but this isn't the main reason the skills shortage has come about. For the UK, the challenges in recruitment and retention, particularly in the public sector, have been fostered by a unique combination of stagnant wages and stagnant investment across the board.

This in turn cascades into the private sector. According to the British Chambers of Commerce, around 60% of companies were looking to recruit staff, but 80% of these companies were also struggling to fill these roles.

Why is there a shortage, though?

In answering this question I'll mostly stick with the UK, as this is the country whose problems on this front I know best, and I think our issues are instructive for everyone regarding how not to grow a skilled workforce.

For there to be a skills shortage now, the number of people leaving the industry must be greater than the number of people joining the industry. This is only exacerbated by the increased demand that the future will bring, particularly for a rail industry that needs to expand quickly.

An immediate cause is the enormous scale of staff retirement without a flow of new trainees to replace them.

This is as much a demographic challenge as it is a training one. Our ageing population means the overall size of the workforce is shrinking. The ratio of working to non-working people is decreasing, and so every sector is competing over a smaller and smaller pool of people. By the mid-2020s, around 20% of engineers and technicians currently working in the UK will have retired. This is stark — without sufficient overlap between new and retiring staff, training is very difficult and the retention of key knowledge is even harder. The problem is further exacerbated by the increased numbers of professionals working from home, making the transfer of experience more difficult still.

## Giving workers hope

We talked about the need to ensure that funding powers are devolved to maximise accountability in Chapter 2.3, but when government deploys zero commitment to the future, is it any wonder that young people are uninterested in taking up a career in the sector? Without a clear view of the future, without a government that visibly cares, and without a pipeline of real work, investing millions in training or research facilities is essentially useless and the skills shortage will never be resolved.

The first step in enabling a workforce with the right skills and size to deliver the railway we need — and indeed this applies to the economy at large — is to create the vision and long-term plan that we've described in the previous chapter. Doing so allows prospective employees to see a future in the sector (an underestimated requirement), allows employers to develop their own recruitment and training campaigns to grow and match the expected pipeline of work, and provides private and public organisations with the confidence to collaborate on developing sufficient capacity to train and develop people to fulfil both their own needs and the needs of the industry.

This is only the start of the story, though. Once the plan is in place, government and industry has to follow through with the publication of and commitment to a visible, transparent pipeline of work (infrastructure, trains, renewal, refurbishment, expansion and so on).

Fixing both the policy itself and the way the public and workforce perceive that policy is key.

Even then, the way that policy is enacted will influence the extent to which people want to join and remain within the industry. Politicians may like announcing projects, and transport appraisal guidelines may be set up to favour projects, but projects are actually the weakest way to deliver most major work on railways. New trains are best delivered not on a one-off basis, but as a large-scale and steady stream of replacements. Electrification, resignalling, track renewals, earthworks and drainage, platform and accessibility corrections: all of these are suited to rolling programmes of work steered by a strategic plan. And rolling programmes are far better for staff: boom and bust can be largely eradicated; strong teams can build up over years; retaining skills and relationships is far easier. Life becomes predictable for many workers in a way that the tendered delivery of many discrete schemes cannot facilitate. Without a long-term plan in place, most young people will never be interested in a career in the railway industry.

Britain typifies this in excruciating style in the form of its — now former — dedicated railway training colleges. In 2014, as part of an industrial strategy that it dropped a year later, the UK government announced that a series of national colleges would be opened, including a railway training college stupidly named the National College for High-Speed Rail or NCHSR (it did not specialise in high-speed rail — I know because I taught there). These were to be "employer-led", to "develop advanced manufacturing, digital, wind energy and creative skills", and were part of a drive to greatly increase the number of apprentices in technical sectors across the country.

Of the seven colleges proposed, two were scrapped within months. Nevertheless, £80m was forthcoming for the rail college, which was to be built as two campuses, one in Birmingham and the other in Doncaster. They launched in 2017, and when I started in 2018, they had barely any students at all. With a capacity for over three thousand students, the school had less than one hundred and was being propped up to the tune of several million pounds a year. (I had a tremendous time teaching here, incidentally, and the students I had the pleasure of introducing to track engineering and risk management are now well embedded in industry and thriving. The college was a good idea!)

By 2019, the pressure was being felt by the college management. The NCHSR was renamed the National College for Advanced Transport and Infrastructure, a totally meaningless name that presumably knocked it entirely out of internet search results. Technical courses were swapped with management courses. It achieved nothing. Student numbers continued to flatline.

Having limped on for another four years and shed most of its staff, the college was dissolved. Millions of pounds had been spent. Two state-of-the-art and genuinely excellent facilities filled with cutting-edge teaching technology, real railway track, full-sized trains and all manner of tools and equipment were abandoned. Dedicated further-education practitioners were made redundant. It was a mess.

A litany of problems led to the college's failure. Its management had no understanding of the railway industry. It had been created by the Department of Business, Energy and Industrial Strategy — now defunct — who had little experience in either education or transport. Consequently, it was not well aligned to the rail industry or its existing ecosystem of training and development institutions. Further to this, the government's deeply cynical agnosticism towards its own high-speed rail project greatly reduced the demand for apprentices.

Most fundamental, though, was the lack of any long-term commitment to a plan for railway investment. Companies will not recruit and train staff if they have no more than a six-month view of the pipeline of work. It is a basic concept that the UK government is incapable of grasping.

They've repeated this over and over again across the country. The electrification college in South Wales was rendered useless when Westminster cancelled electrification of the South Wales Main Line beyond Cardiff. The Tunnelling and Underground Construction Academy in London, built for Crossrail with the intention of being used for Crossrail 2 and the expansion of the London Underground system, has lain dormant since Crossrail's tunnelling contracts concluded thanks to central government withdrawing all but tick-over funding from Transport for London.

It's a similar story for research and development. Perhaps the most excruciating example is the Very Light Rail National Innovation Centre in Dudley in the West Midlands. The £32m facility was built for testing urban very light rail (VLR) — an underwhelming reinvention of a diminutive vintage streetcar, but made of plastic and with fewer seats — and opened in 2022.

The VLR concept may be a dud, but the Dudley facilities do genuinely provide the opportunity for useful testing of more conventional tram systems. However, despite being set up to facilitate another West Midlands city's deployment of urban VLR (Coventry wanted to see VLR running in 2024), the site has been underused (to put it mildly). This is only going to get worse given the Department for

Transport rejected Coventry's first major funding bid. The UK government loves spending millions on research and development, but funding permanent transport infrastructure, particularly local or urban systems, is anathema.

To build the workforce we need in order to deliver the future, rail can and should be a model for improving workers' rights, optimising management techniques and structures, managing change, supporting worker welfare and competency, maintaining sustainable and ethical business practices and much more. Indeed, railways can already be instructive on some of these fronts. As we've already described, they also fail on many of them.

In too many parts of the world, the power of collective bargaining is being eroded, not bolstered. To overcome the skills gap and build a workforce that is happy, healthy, valued and safe requires this trend be reversed.

Suggestions that higher union membership and empowerment lead to a worse railway don't stand up to scrutiny. History has shown, again and again, that only the collective action of an organised workforce can ensure conditions, pay and safety are maintained.

It is easy to muddle the wider workforce statistics in relation to the safety of unionised and non-unionised workers. Broadly, unionised workers tend to be those working on physically demanding, dangerous worksites, and who are exposed to higher levels of risk than their non-unionised colleagues, who (again, broadly) tend to work in less-risky, white-collar roles. Care must therefore be taken when understanding the impact of union involvement on worker safety.

Nevertheless, the effect of unions on health, safety and wellbeing is well researched and significant. Safety is a higher priority for union members than pay — indeed, the UK's Trades Union Congress has consistently reported that safety is one of the main reasons that people join a union, and union membership has been associated strongly with improved worker safety in successive research papers up to the present day. This is true for ill-health and injuries, and it is even more true for fatalities. A 2013 analysis across 31 countries concluded that "union density is the most important external determinant of workplace psychosocial safety climate, health and GDP".[3] Unions keep their members — and other non-union members working in unionised workplaces — safer.

It isn't just the dramatic, gory stuff that unions protect their staff from: unions were among the first organisations to raise awareness of workplace stress and mental wellbeing. Long-term health risks from asbestos and fine dusts were first raised by unions, too.

Even the UK government itself has calculated that union action to improve safety and wellbeing means economic gains of as much as £1bn per year in today's prices (this figure has been estimated to be as high as £1.6bn in further research using government figures).

Though they have had a mixed history with diversity over the years, unions have generally stood in solidarity with women, people of colour and the LGBTQ+ community. In the mid-1970s, tens of thousands of marchers were brought out by the unions to support exploited women, mostly of South Asian descent, in the Grunwick strikes in northwest London. In the late 1980s, unions protested strongly against the UK government's violently homophobic Section 28 legislation — strong ties had already been forged between striking mineworkers and LGBT activist groups. Research across the world has shown a consistent, strong

---

[3] Maureen Dollard and Daniel Neser (2013) "Worker Health Is Good for the Economy" Social Science and Medicine, Volume 92, September, Pages 114–123.

link between union membership and support for policies that benefit minority populations, including in the USA.

Today, unions continue to provide support for people from LGBTQ+ backgrounds to work freely and without discrimination — increasing their wellbeing and ensuring they remain satisfied and comfortable within their industry.

On the flip side, contracting companies working on major projects in the UK have commonly enacted anti-union policies, even up to the present day. In doing so, they threaten the safety of their workers as well as worsening their working conditions.

In November 2023, *Tribune* magazine reported on claims by the UK's Unite construction union that workers on High Speed 2 sites that operate anti-union policies are more than three times more likely to be involved in accidents than workers on the unionised site of Hinkley Point C (the UK's first new nuclear power station in several decades). This is the wrong way to build a railway, and particularly one that is so crucial to Britain's future.

A safer site is a more efficient site, as you avoid the step-downs and pauses arising from close-call safety events or — in the worst circumstances — injuries or deaths. The health and wellbeing feedback that unions can provide improves the productivity of the workforce and increases retention of staff in the longer term. All of this means you deliver more stuff per person working for you — which means, ultimately, we build the railway we need more quickly.

The idea that an organisation or project can bypass these benefits and reduce costs by relying on non-union workers is false: more accidents, lower worker retention and the broader costs to the construction industry of having to train more people to account for those who leave — due to injury, long-term health issues or worse — wipe out any wage savings.

For the tech industry, 2023 was a pivotal year for unionisation and labour organising. As the pandemic tech boom slowed (among other things), investors lost the code to the infinite money cheat, meaning less money was flying in the direction of tech companies. All of a sudden, the almightiest tech companies were laying off thousands of staff. In January 2023, Google laid off twelve thousand of its workers. Facebook shed eleven thousand. Amazon laid off eighteen thousand. For staff who weren't sacked, their snazzy benefits started disappearing, presumably including beanbags and free lychees (in all seriousness, tech industry working conditions were already bad, and they took a dive in 2022–23).

All of a sudden, working for these companies didn't make you untouchable, and the value of collective organising was felt as sharply as a pin prick. After the Google layoffs, hundreds of staff joined the embryonic Alphabet Workers Union. It's a picture that's emerging across the sector.

Workers that are downstream of the tech giants themselves have also been organising. As the so-called "gig economy" has pushed yet more people into precarious roles, those people have responded as best they can by organising, either by joining existing unions or creating their own.

The GMB Union in the UK has swept up and supported staff pushed into precarious, contingent or otherwise exploitative contracts by tech industry "innovation". For example, a landmark case confirming that Uber drivers are indeed classified as workers and deserve minimum working conditions was brought by drivers with the assistance of the union. Similar cases have been brought against other companies.

Even closer to the frontline, the Independent Workers Union of Great Britain was founded by migrant cleaners in 2012 and has been increasingly organising gig economy workers and others pushed to the edge of reasonable working conditions by tech industry efficiency. Its numbers have swollen into the thousands, covering outsourced staff, charity workers and even those in the tech industry itself.

Meanwhile, the picture is very different in the railway, where union membership continues to decline.

It's hard to tell precisely what percentage of the UK rail industry is unionised, as large numbers of people, including private-sector workers, are not classified as railway staff in the official statistics. The official figure of 70% in 2021 is thus likely to be an overcount given private-sector workers are much less likely to be unionised in the UK.

One of the challenges for labour organising in the railway industry is that not only has collective action been battered to within an inch of existence by the punitive anti-union laws in places like the UK, but large swathes of the industry aren't in a union and don't see a place for union membership at all. As roles in the industry shift, the spaces which organised workers inhabit are being squeezed out of existence.

One upside in the railways for building union membership is that organised staff very visibly receive better pay and conditions than non-unionised staff.

Unions provide one voice in the workplace, highlighting the ideal working conditions for their members and thus providing an easy blueprint for employers to follow. Without unions to provide a buffer against unfavourable or uncomfortable (let alone unsafe) working conditions, individualised staff become less productive and achieve less in the time they are being paid.

Obviously this is a liberal-framed argument, though. Unions are the most powerful tool for pushing employers and industries to improve their working practices to create a happier workforce, proud (and keen) to work in the roles they do.

The four-day working week is not a new idea, but recent trials in the UK have shown that — without reducing salaries — it improves staff retention and productivity, therefore reducing costs. Unions and campaigners have been at the forefront of making the case for these trials, and such innovations in working conditions can and should be prioritised in the rail industry to further incentivise people to join and stay in it. In turn, these innovations can then benefit other industries and domains.

There are countless examples of railway workers leading the way in pushing forwards rights and conditions for the rest of us, but my favourite led to the creation of a British institution we can be proud of, despite its myriad contemporary failings: the National Health Service.

As the Great Western Railway (GWR) between London and Bristol was being built, Swindon was selected as the location of its locomotive and rolling stock works. Building and maintaining trains was hard, heavy, dangerous work, and the manual labour resulted in a lot of injuries.

By 1847, the Great Western Railway Medical Fund Society was founded, following a plea from the locomotive superintendent of the railway works to the board of the company. All workers would pay a small subscription, and free medical care would be provided to staff and their families by a local doctor.

The fund quickly developed into a body campaigning for improved living conditions and sanitation in Swindon. Baths were opened and expanded in the workshops. The fund opened its own hospital in 1871, and Britain's first medical centre in 1892.

As the Second World War was won, many tens of thousands of sick and injured people returned to the country. With the scale of effort required to rebuild and modernise the country, it was seen that state welfare and health services would be required. The man charged with creating the new health service was Aneurin Bevan.

Of the GWR Medical Fund, he said simply: "There it was, a complete health service. All we had to do was to expand it to embrace the whole country." And so he did. In 1947, a century after its founding, the GWR Medical Fund was wound up. In its place, the National Health Service sprang forth and provided medical care for all, free at the point of use.

The railway unions can and do act to tie together the fragmented national railway industries that liberalisation has created, providing links between infrastructure staff keeping tracks maintained, signalling staff controlling trains, guards keeping passengers safe and drivers ensuring they are moving. They shine a light on unsafe working conditions where patterns are seen to be emerging, and keep managers honest as constant reorganisations and efficiency drives allow hard-won safety practices to be forgotten. They can help shift organisations and their workers through times of change — including changes in technology and working practices.

The unions aren't perfect; as with any organised power structure, they have to act to protect themselves. Any given organised power structure will also reflect the challenges of the society it represents. However, their membership structure ensures that they are representative of the needs of working people and provide a democratic mandate to their leaders and spokespeople.

## Giving workers knowledge

Unions can help protect and retain the skilled people our future needs, but how do those people know what skills they need in the first place? How does industry retain the knowledge it has, facilitate the passage of that knowledge between people and domains and understand how knowledge and skills need to change for the future?

A long-term lack of investment in secondary school education is a deep-rooted cause of the skills shortage. Reductions in pay and the quality of working conditions, as well as increased demands on specialist secondary teaching staff, mean that there are fewer university-educated teachers (or those with equivalent experience), reducing the overall quality of teaching as well as distancing students from the industries their subjects are useful in. If you are teaching a subject at or in some cases above the level you've been trained in yourself, you are unlikely to provide an engaging teaching experience.

The demise of apprenticeships is another major contributor. Providing a pathway into technical roles that doesn't involve tens of thousands of pounds of university debt would seem like a no-brainer, and many people are choosing this route into technical roles today via modern apprenticeship programmes. However, the numbers as a percentage of the UK population are an order of magnitude below where they were in the mid-1960s, when around a third of school leavers went into an apprenticeships (this picture is reflected across Europe). The all-time low was reached in the early 1990s, with only 53,000 apprentices training in the UK in 1990.

Furthermore, looking at the rail industry in particular, both apprenticeship and graduate programmes were coordinated directly by the nationalised state railway organisation British Rail before its privatisation in the 1990s. If you wanted a job in the railways, you knew where to go. Those schemes were generalised, giving trainees the chance to understand the full industry and the importance of every single role within it. The railways are a system, and while you don't need to understand every part to work in it, it helps to at least have an appreciation of that systemic nature and the relationships within it.

Indeed, there's an argument to be had that the last cohorts of the British Rail graduate scheme are the ones holding today's railway industry together, given the number of strategic roles held across the country by those who were part of the scheme in its last years. As their numbers diminish, so too will the unique and valuable system-wide understanding that they draw upon — replacing whole-industry training schemes is vital to retaining this skillset.

Today, apprenticeship scheme numbers are climbing, albeit not to historic levels, but knowing where to find them and how applicable they are to your desired role — or if they will trap you in a role you don't have much interest in — is difficult.

Graduates are also not being equipped with the required skills to take on technical — and, crucially, systemic — roles. Indeed, the feedback on graduate recruitment quality is generally that where a lack of technical capability can be backfilled; it is the lack of "soft-skills" (a phrase I admittedly do not like) that causes the deepest issues for employers. As students are pushed further towards examinations over other means of grade monitoring, their ability to learn to communicate and work with others is diminished.

In the UK, the university sector was expected to pick up the pieces following the demise of British Rail and its training and research capabilities. For training, this simply hasn't worked. There are almost no top-tier university courses in railway engineering, railway planning or railway management. In fact, the importance of the railway as an employer in all types of engineering is barely reflected in the offerings of higher education. Only the University of Birmingham offers an undergraduate course that mentions railway engineering in its title.

I've talked a lot here about technical roles, but the skills shortage is not and must not be seen as one bounded only by STEM subjects. Indeed, STEM has long been used as a tool to commodify education, channel workers into economically desirable, non-unionised jobs and reduce funding for humanities subjects. As a framework for bringing people into railway engineering roles, it is as unhelpful as its initialisation, which makes no sense at all given technology isn't a subject, science includes basically everything (including a lot of people on salaries far below the median wage for graduates) and engineering and mathematics aren't exactly parallel fields either. Attempts to add the letter "A" to make it STEAM and include the arts are even more baffling and insulting, both to the arts and to engineering (engineering is creative already!). And that's before we talk about the origin of pro-STEM policy as a largely US-based response to the idea that its economy was being increasingly out-competed by highly educated Chinese students especially capable in maths and technology — a policymakers' trope steeped in orientalist prejudice.

People involved in delivering STEM initiatives are almost invariably well meaning, but the use of this moniker has done nothing to plug the skills gap in the years since it has been deployed, and it has been used by governments, universities, colleges and other authorities as an excuse to devalue some people's chosen vocation — in many cases providing "justification" for contracting out or closing down humanities roles and departments.

The reality is that STEM initiatives result in doors into engineering being closed, not opened. The idea that you need to have completed a STEM degree to be a capable or competent engineering practitioner is patently false. Indeed, the sector needs more people with a more diverse range of interests and capabilities, not least in language, graphic design and social sciences.

Further to all of this, detaching science and engineering from the humanities and the ethical structures required to develop and apply science and engineering principles is a dangerous misstep. Through history, engineers have consistently been the ones to make the most significant changes to the safety and wellbeing of humanity — positive or indeed negative. The greatest improvements to life expectancy have come from the widespread provision of safe drinking water, heating and lighting. At the same time, motorised transport accounts for over a million deaths annually, making road traffic collisions the leading cause of death for children and young adults globally. Climate change represents the single greatest threat to life on earth, and it is engineers who have provided the technologies that spew greenhouse gases into the atmosphere.

Sustainability is about far more than environmental issues: transport inequality, prejudice, discrimination and societal change all impact on the railway industry, and in turn engineers impact them. I define sustainability as a question: Will the choices we make now be the right ones in the future? To make sustainable choices, engineering practitioners need to understand what challenges the future will bring, and how those challenges should influence their choices. Engineers cannot be expected to be experts in all of these fields, yet they have to make decisions that impact all of them. Given this enormous responsibility, and the clear impacts that such decisions can have on billions of lives, does a STEM-focused education prepare engineers appropriately? Are engineers being provided with a framework within which to determine if the decisions they make are the right ones?

As evidenced by the slow pace of greenhouse gas emission reductions, the continued expansion of highway networks and the pursuit of technologies that will worsen all of the metrics they are supposed to be improving, I would suggest that the answer to that question is a resounding no; engineers are left to fend for themselves, meaning that without malice or ill intent, the wrong decisions are repeatedly being made.

I ran a (reasonably unscientific) poll with a reasonable circulation back in 2021 asking, "If you were taught engineering of any kind at university, which of the following options covers the ethics training you received?" to which 16% said they had attended a dedicated course, 25% said they had attended one or two lectures, and a whopping 59% said that ethics had been hardly or not mentioned at all.

Whether it is via a university degree, college or an apprenticeship, engineers are not being suitably prepared to understand the context within which their knowledge is applied. This vacuum risks being filled by non-moral decision frameworks, leaving engineers to make choices based only on engineering expediency, cost or political whimsy.

Without ethical training, and without the ethical frameworks established by those practicing the humanities, engineers and engineering practitioners are doomed to compound the problems society is facing.

Engineers cannot pass the buck onto policymakers and politicians — they should take great pride in the influence their expertise has had on society, but they should also take responsibility for it.

Any company, college or country can run a STEM initiative, and it will get marginal results at best. Meanwhile, without a clear strategy from government, people will not train for an industry without a visible future.

For anyone looking to start or change their career, in the railway or otherwise, there is an enormous plethora of skills and training initiatives, none of which are coordinated, few of which are audited to evaluate their success, and all of which lack the power to drive any meaningful change. Unsurprisingly, an economic framework that is set up to ensure that nothing material happens is incapable of making anything material happen.

## Defragmenting the industry

Whether via the impact on education and training initiatives or in allowing new entrants into the industry to get a holistic picture of how the railway works, we can see how fragmentation of an industry and the homogenisation of pathways into that industry are key obstacles to recruitment.

By way of a warning to the world, there can be no greater obstacle to maximising the pool of available talent than the aggressive outsourcing regime pursued by the British railway industry, which in turn prevents the open flow of skilled people within the industry.

Facilities-management staff, train cleaners, on-site safety staff and even some station staff — invariably those on the lowest wages and in the most precarious roles — are not employed by the rail companies or even their major contractors. These people are employed by outsourcing agencies, ensuring that their pay and working conditions can be more easily squeezed and that labour organising is more difficult. Relevant to growing our workforce, staff in these roles are more likely to struggle with attainment at school and to afford college or university.

Where these roles would have historically offered another route into the industry, in today's fragmented and outsourced industry no such pathway is available. We are choosing to close down routes into skilled roles rather than widen and diversify the pool of talent our industry has access to. Unless you are shaping an industry around short-term frontier extraction rather than delivery of a public service, it makes no sense and must be reversed.

To build the right workforce to unleash the potential of the railways, we need to tackle the skills shortage by laying out what the railways need to look like. To keep the current and future workforce safe, comfortable and in control of their destinies, we need to increase union membership and involvement in the railways. And to ensure that those same staff are able to access and share knowledge, we need strong professional institutions embedded in the railway industry.

Get this right — planning for the future, growing collective worker power and minimising outsourcing — and you'll set up the railways as a core employer as the latest wave of automation pushes society into the biggest era of employment change it has seen since financialisaton, if not since industrialisation.

# CHAPTER 2.6

# AUTOMATE WITH CARE

Automation hasn't just been deployed by the railways through their history — the railways gave the world commercial electronics and light-speed communication.

Far from being a follower when it comes to the *useful* application of automation, the railways have been and continue to be in the forefront of technological capability, acting as a pathfinder for other sectors when it comes to what works and what is junk.

However, today's surge in automation is being led by the tech industry's latest fixation — artificial intelligence. Do not be fooled: the tools being deployed under this moniker are anything but intelligent. The threat they represent is not existential doom at the hands of our machine overlords; rather, it's precisely the same threat every form of automation has presented since the start of the industrial revolution. The reason the brokers of these various evolving and emerging technologies want us to see the threat as something out of a science fiction dystopia is that regulators will be accordingly distracted, freeing them up to get on with deploying AI to undercut and make redundant existing workers.

Today, AI differs from previous forms of automation in that it is reaching into the previously safe realms of the stenographer and the spreadsheet jockey. For economies built on the service industry, tools misleadingly labelled as "AI" represent a serious threat to economic and social stability because — despite promises to the contrary for two centuries or more — automation in the hands of incumbent power structures will not result in our having lots of free time to enjoy life and to better ourselves. What it will actually mean is greatly increased precarity for millions more workers across the globe, including those white-collar workers who may previously have felt secure.

## Railways gave us the electronic age

Straightening out his collars, William Fothergill Cooke walked through the small assembly to a diminutive desk with a wooden chair tucked slightly underneath. The wooden floorboards creaked as he took slow, purposeful steps. The room smelled like fresh timber and paint, having only recently been erected, but there was also a rising scent of burning coal entering by means of a door to the rear.

Cooke was aware that the men surrounding him were not the dignitaries joining his colleague Professor Charles Wheatstone a mile or so south, but nevertheless he felt their gaze as hotly. A few were foremen of the railway company, who'd found a moment's pause in their work to steal a glance at an unusual device that had taken shape over the preceding few weeks. One was a man of the press, a writer for a scientific periodical of some kind, who had pushed his way to the front of the small crowd. Perhaps the keenest gaze, though, was that of the resident engineer of the company, a man called Fox.

Having passed the journalist, who was holding the nub end of a pencil above a notebook, Cooke drew back the chair and sat himself in it, pausing for a moment to glance out of the darkened window at the shadows of two tremendous chimneys, each belching an indecisive cough of smoke high into the still Camden skies. Below these, glinting in the light of nearby gas lamps and the high moon, were eight strips of steel, dropping down out of sight into the depths of a great, brick-lined excavation.

Drawing himself back into the moment, Cooke reached for a wooden contraption, about the size of a jewellery box, connected by around a dozen separate, wound-metal filaments that disappeared under the table. He took a short breath and pressed two of the finger levers jutting out of the wooden box forwards. Despite it being July, they were cold to the touch.

He then shifted himself slightly in the chair to ensure his audience had a view of a tall board, varnished and with a diamond cut into it. Behind that diamond was an enamel panel upon which protruded five needles. The panel also included letters of the alphabet that two of the five needles would briefly point to, allowing messages to be transmitted that would, as Cooke understood it, dictate the actions the foremen were to take in operating a large rope-and-pulley system to haul passenger and goods wagons up from the railway's terminus at Euston Square. The two great chimneys each sat above a stationary steam engine, with both connected to this system. The smoke they created travelled little in the cold night air, hence the smokiness swirling around him and his small band of interested individuals.

The tension in the room elevated.

Cooke considered what his next words might be should no response be forthcoming. He was just short of opening his mouth when a sudden click punctured the silence. Two of the needles on the tall board shifted from vertical to pointing inwards towards a letter. Then another pair pointed to another letter. And so on. As the letters assembled into a word, followed by another word, Cooke read them out. They soon formed an instruction.

Behind him, one of the foremen strode across the room and started spinning a large wheel in his hands, and the sound of steam entering a piston filled the room.

This noise was loud enough to drown out the calls of excitement from the crowd, but Cooke had heard enough to know he had satisfied the onlookers. He had achieved what he needed to. He and his partner had transmitted electrical signals to each other along metal wires he had earlier laid along the track — the age of commercial telegraphy, and indeed of practical electronics, had begun.

Later, the engineer called Fox (Charles Fox, who the following year would become the inventor of mechanical railway points used to connect converging or diverging tracks) would write to Cooke as follows:

> I have great pleasure in adding my testimony to that of many others, who have been gratified by witnessing the very beautiful experiments exhibited by yourself and Professor Wheatstone to prove the practicability of transmitting signals by means of electro-magnetic fluid. Nothing can have been more satisfactory than these experiments, which have placed beyond a doubt that the principle may be applied with unerring certainty.[4]

The date had been 25 July 1837, and the London and Birmingham Railway had just instigated the beginning of the age of commercial light-speed communication.

Three companies had operating arrangements to bring trains into Euston. The Grand Junction Railway linked the London and Birmingham with the Liverpool and Manchester railways (this was the UK's burgeoning

---

[4] Charles Wheatstone (1855) *A Reply to Mr. Cooke's Pamphlet*, London, Richard Taylor and William Francis

intercity network, and it is no coincidence that it also forms the backbone of its current, if hobbled, high-speed aspirations). In what would certainly not be the last example of private commercial interfaces stifling innovation, the lack of interest from the Grand Junction in laying Cooke and Wheatstone's telegraph wires along their right of way meant that the directors of the London and Birmingham Railway saw no value in laying the wires northwards to the limits of their own line.

Until the merger of the three companies into the London and North-Western Railway in 1846, the short section of telegraph remained in situ, but was only operated for six months before being replaced by a more primitive pipe with a whistle on the end.

It was another two years before a permanent application of the technology began operation on the Great Western Railway in December 1839 as a primitive form of electronic block signalling. By 1846 the newly formed London and North-Western Railway was lifting telegraph circuits on poles to enable use of an advancement and simplification of the previous systems. Unlike its predecessors, this system was a dedicated electronic signalling system. The same year, Cooke bought out his academic colleague and founded the Electric Telegraph Company (ETC), the first in the world, with the intention of making the system publicly available.

The ETC remained the largest British telegraph company until the whole system was nationalised in 1870, becoming part of the General Post Office. GPO telecommunications engineers would lead the design of the world's first programmable, electronic, digital computer — Colossus — from 1943 as part of the Bletchley code-breaking efforts. In 1969, a separate telecommunications department was created within the Post Office, and in 1981 it was spun out as British Telecoms, before being privatised.

The international expansion of the telegraph was spearheaded not by the ETC's technology, though, but by Samuel Morse and his collaborators in the US. Again, this system relied on the cables raised on poles alongside the railroads.

Not only was technological innovation harnessed by the railways, but the telecommunication industry — and therefore the tech industry — in fact owes its existence to the need for the railways to innovate. Telegraphy was a necessary innovation to better maintain the space between trains and so improve the safety.

The connections run deeper. In the 1880s, Herman Hollerith (formerly of the Massachusetts Institute of Technology) drew inspiration from seeing railroad tickets being punched, and created a machine capable of processing punched cards via electromechanical means. Though the use of punched cards in automated systems was nothing new, Hollerith's machine would beat the competition to process the data from the 1890 US census, and only five years later the New York Central Railroad was the first private commercial user. Railroad usage rapidly increased, given the need for the railways to process enormous volumes of repetitive data.

These early computational devices would become equally as popular in the UK from 1905, when the first system was adopted by the Lancashire and Yorkshire Railway. Nineteen years later, and following success largely driven by the railroad business, Hollerith's company would be renamed IBM. Its UK wholesaler — which would later go on to manufacture the "bombes" for Alan Turing's early code-breaking efforts — found the British railway industry to be by far its largest customer base.

In turn, the cutting-edge application of computer hardware to engineering problem-solving in the 1960s allowed Dr Alan Wickens and his British Rail Research

Department boffins to solve the hunting problem and unleash high-speed rail on the world. The same year that Wickens joined British Rail, the Research Department trialled the use of barcodes as a way to control wagon movements, beating supermarkets in their use by twelve years. Again, in 1962, British Rail's Pegasus 2 digital computer was the first in the world to generate a railway timetable.

As tech's telecoms age transitioned into the internet age, its relationship with railways has only been embedded further, with the US internet infrastructure in particular tied closely to the railroad network. These two systems of physically interconnected lines grew thanks to the same mixture of laissez-faire yet readily cash-backed government input. There's a reason the terms "online" and "offline" originate from railroad usage.

## Capital versus automation

Almost every night shift I've ever worked starts with a long wait in the car, drinking Irn-Bru, glancing at the safety paperwork and otherwise twiddling my thumbs. Occasionally someone will wander over to ask a few questions, but for the most part, there will be at least an hour of dithering before my little team and I are able to have our briefing and step on track.

There are two reasons for this.

The first is because — as someone not doing any major physical work to the railway and essentially just walking about on it, scribbling pencil marks in a notebook, taking photos, rubbing chalk on bits of it and kicking others — my work usually slides down the priority list versus other overnight activities that might be going on nearby.

The second reason is more pertinent, though, because on a railway that harnesses automation from top to bottom, it shows how much space there still is to streamline working practices. In order to facilitate safe access onto the railway for me and whoever I am working with, a safe system of work has to be established, often utilising a possession of the line to keep people and moving trains well apart from each other. This requires quite a bit of preparatory paperwork, meetings and so on, but things essentially kick off when the person in charge of the possession — the PICOP — contacts the signaller to tell them what the plan is. The signaller then gets back in touch once the line is clear of traffic, possibly hours later if trains have been delayed. A back and forth over forms will then follow, with the signaller giving the PICOP permission to take the line.

The PICOP then places a possession limit board and six little explosive detonators in advance of them at each end of the possession, then calls the signaller back (who may be busy with lots of other things going on), who grants permission for the possession to proceed once they are happy correct protection has been applied.

All this time, I'm still sat in the car. And there's more to be done yet.

At this point, the PICOP briefs the various engineering supervisors (they have various official names these days) leading worksites within their possession. These engineering supervisors then go off and place their worksite marker boards down to keep different working parties separated to avoid machines running people over and other calamities.

Having done this, they confirm with the PICOP, who then gives them their worksite. And even now, things aren't yet complete. Each engineering supervisor then briefs each of the controllers of site safety, who are in charge of keeping individual working teams safe within the worksite. In turn, they then brief the working teams.

Only then can the teams actually doing stuff on the railway step on track.

These processes have helped reduce worker fatalities by orders of magnitude in the decades since they were introduced by British Rail. However, they're not time-efficient, and time is the second-most-valuable resource when doing anything on the railway, after the skilled people doing the task itself. Here, then, is a perfect opportunity to introduce improved safe-access procedures given the automation and centralisation of signalling and traction power control. There are potentially millions of annual working hours to be saved.

And so it is for many aspects of today's railway operation.

Cooke and Wheatstone's telegraph was one of the earliest form of electronic automation. For the railways, this was only the very start of a process of automation that continues today. Very quickly, the technology was used to enable trains to work more closely together while improving safety by creating a block system by which trains would be allowed into a section of track by a signaller communicating with their colleague along the line. This was refined and rolled out across increasing lengths of the railway network, but its total application was usually stymied by railway company thrift.

Later, lineside signals would emerge as an indication to drivers that the railway was clear ahead of them. Originally, these were simply activated by a signaller who had to ensure that the signal matched reality. Further development would, by 1856, incorporate cut-metal interlockings that would lock signal positions and the arrangements of track points (where tracks converge and diverge) to avoid conflicting signals. These interlockings would become so enormous and complex as routes grew and diversified that they would evolve from mechanical to electro-mechanical to electrical relay systems which would themselves influence the development of computers. The railway companies, however, were often not the instigators of such advancements.

On a pleasant Sunday in June of 1889, near the county town of Armagh in today's Northern Ireland, an excursion train packed with children on their way to the seaside was struggling to ascend one of the steep gradients on the secondary line to Newry.

The locomotive was underpowered for the size of train, and it failed to reach the top, stalling a matter of metres before the summit. The train crew decided to take the first five coaches of fifteen on to a station over the crest of the hill and return for the rest. Owing to a primitive design, the splitting of the train would mean the ten coaches would be relying on the handbrakes in the brake van at the rear of the train. With these applied and pieces of ballast used to scotch the wheels of the coaches, the shorter front part of the train made off.

In doing so, it nudged the rear portion such that the wheels rode over the scotching stones and left all ten, fully loaded coaches resting on the single brake in the van.

This was hopelessly inadequate. The weight quickly overcame the van's handbrake and the rear portion of the train started to run back down the hill. The line was worked not by the block system but by a time-interval system which assumed that a train would pass through a section within a set time and would then allow the following train through. Consequently, the next train — a scheduled passenger train — was already making its way up the gradient at pace.

The driver of that train saw the oncoming carriages and stopped his own, which in the subsequent collision was mostly unharmed.

The excursion train did not fare so well. It struck the locomotive of the ascending train with such force that its rear coaches were totally destroyed, killing or severely injuring 340 people, most of whom were children.

The staff operating the train — including the driver, who had originally complained about having to operate such a long train with a small locomotive — were prosecuted for manslaughter, though their cases were later dropped.

Senior management at the Great Northern Railway (Ireland) company escaped any judgement whatsoever, despite their inadequate equipment and infrastructure being the root cause of the crash. Nevertheless, it was clearly stated in the subsequent inquest that the presence of automatic continuous brakes would have prevented the collision, as would absolute block signalling.

What happened next was a key moment in railway and corporate history. Parliament rushed to pass legislation that would mandate lock, block and brake (that is, signal interlocking, absolute block and fail-safe automatic continuous brakes) for all passenger railway operations. With some deep reticence, the railway companies complied. The age when they did as they pleased was over. The age when government would increasingly step in to regulate and control railway operations had begun.

The 1889 Regulation of Railways Act greatly reduced the number of railway accidents occurring on the railways of Britain and Ireland. Private enterprise had been unwilling to exploit technology for good other than where it suited them, and the state stepped in to force their hand. It wouldn't be the last time this happened, either on railways or in broader society. Laissez-faire was coming to an end.

Today, the era of the lone signaller in their box is largely over, as centralised signalling control centres using electronic (and more recently solid-state) interlocking have taken over.

## Mechanisation and safety

Automation takes other forms, too. On track, the reduction in human effort and labour was mostly termed mechanisation, as trains designed to drop and shape ballast on the tracks replaced armies of men with bars, picks and shovels.

The innovation feeding mechanisation built up pace in the inter-war years, as pressures from alternative modes was pushing revenue harder and the availability of manual labourers was waning. However, it was the massive downwards pressure on the availability of labour in the aftermath of the Second World War that accelerated mechanisation dramatically. Industry at large was short of men.

One consequence of this was a massive migration of workers from Britain's current and former colonies, not least from the Caribbean and Indian subcontinent. Another consequence, though, was extreme pressure to mechanise more maintenance and construction tasks on the railways.

A veritable menagerie of on-track machines followed, with Austria generally taking the lead in the development of these. Without them, the railways would simply not have been able to function. As a result, the number of workers per mile of railway has halved since 1948 from twelve to six. Reducing the labour intensity, and thus cost, of maintenance and renewal is a laudable endeavour. Less money spent on one element of maintenance means more to spend on another, and less spent on maintenance overall means more for renewal or enhancements, increasing rail's capacity and its ability to deliver everything we've already talked about.

But there's another factor at play. The more staff you have on track doing manual labour, the more injuries and negative health outcomes (dust inhalation, musculoskeletal problems, etc.) your workforce incurs. It has historically meant more worker fatalities, too. So mechanisation and automation to take boots off ballast is a positive thing for worker safety.

I've been lucky enough to ride in the cab of trains travelling at 200 km/h along Britain's East Coast Main Line, and the immediate thing that struck me was the level of trust required to hold the whole railway together. At the speeds modern trains operate at, avoiding hitting an obstacle requires the driver to brake before they've seen it, which is plainly impossible without assistance. Thus maintaining that trust is crucial.

With so many moving parts, inspection of the railway to ensure everything is as it should be is crucial.

In the past, such inspections were carried out on foot, as often as morning and night. With more trains running, this became infeasible. Regular inspections moved from eye level on track to cameras and instruments mounted on special trains. These instruments began as analogue needles leaving marks on pieces of paper, but the computer age allowed these to be automated, then digitised.

If inspection technologies leapt forwards towards the end of the twentieth century, then our ability to analyse that data has jumped forwards commensurately in the 2010s. Unlike many purported areas of application for so-called artificial intelligence technologies, the nature of the railways as long strings of highly repeatable elements makes them well suited to such innovations.

Network Rail's world-leading plain-line pattern-recognition train captures 70,000 images a second, travelling at 200 km/h. Its high-resolution images capture every millimetre of the railway in sufficient detail to identify almost all visible defects quickly, and with more accuracy than the regular human visual inspections that they replaced. This is thanks to the well-tested use of machine learning to identify not just common defects but unusual ones.

With over ten terabytes of visual data per shift (that's twice a day) being collected alongside countless other traces and metrics, the opportunity to predict as well as react to defects is enormous. The use-cases are only limited by the size of the teams managing the data.

Thanks to a constant shortage of skilled people, and in an environment that is inherently unsafe, railways have created and indeed pioneered forms of automation in technology and operations.

## Problems first, not solutions

When it comes to automation on the railway, I think most people you ask will jump straight to the implementation of driverless trains. I've already alluded to the fact that, when it comes to public transport, the words "driverless" and "autonomous" are usually being used to mask other deficiencies, but the debate over driverless trains ticks two of my "keen interest" boxes. Not only does this subject involve technology for the sake of technology rather than as a means to an end, it also covers accessibility and the safety of passengers at the platform-train interface. (PTI)

Let's look at grades of train automation, or GoA levels. These are the most widely applied means of understanding the extent to which a railway system can be considered "driverless".

Perhaps counterintuitively, the best way to understand each level is to look at what the on-train person (be they a driver or attendee) still has to do. At GoA1, the driver has to start and stop the train to its schedule and operate the doors (among other things). At GoA2, the driver only has to operate the doors.

GoA3 is where the driver can leave the cab and act only as an attendee: they still operate the doors, though. To take the on-train person off the train entirely requires GoA4, where automation not only takes care of routine starting/stopping and door operations at stations, but must also be able to account for any unplanned circumstances the train might encounter. So while GoA3 has no driver in a cab, only GoA4 can be considered truly driverless.

Whenever a technology-led proposal is put forwards, the first question everyone should ask is always: "What problem will it solve?" and if the list is very short, then that technical proposal is likely to be without merit. That is certainly the case for driverless private cars, but is it true for driverless trains?

Well, because the ability to operate a train entirely without an on-train person is really a question of managing PTI risk, not entirely.

The enabling infrastructure for GoA4 (or indeed full GoA3) would result in greatly reduced risk at the PTI because removing train attendees requires all platforms to be set to standard offsets to enable level boarding and to be fitted with platform edge doors (PEDs). It would also require all trains to be built with low floors to match the platform offsets and to be fitted with automatic gap fillers to deal with platform curvature.

Internationally, the risk at the PTI remains significant. In Britain, it is the only passenger risk that is not improving over time, with the number of PTI-associated fatalities and injuries still increasing year on year. The PTI improvements associated with the shift to GoA4 would not only improve safety, they would also greatly improve accessibility, and can create capacity improvements by reducing dwell times (the time a train spends at a platform).

The fitting of PEDs would also greatly reduce the number of suicides on the system (as well as less-frequent accidental deaths from people falling off platforms), in turn reducing trauma for station staff.

However, in most systems this will not necessarily translate into greater capacity or journey time improvements. Why? For lower-density systems, perhaps interurban or regional railways, the limits on capacity do not generally stem from dwell times. Limits on track capacity, particularly for mixed-traffic railways, result from the number of trains able to traverse junctions or other bottlenecks, from the patterns of stopping and non-stopping trains through intermediate stations, or from differential speeds between different trains. Driverless trains do not resolve this; improved track layouts, better signalling and homogenisation of services patterns do.

For urban systems, pushing more trains per hour along a given track does not account for the ability of people to get from the street, through the station, onto the platform and into the train. The bottleneck moves from the track into the station, and in the case of the major urban interchanges in cities across the world, these often-underground labyrinths have already reached excruciating levels of congestion.

What's more, GoA4 isn't needed to maximise track utilisation: London's Victoria line, for example, operates thirty-six trains per hour under GoA2. This translates to an immense system capacity of 43,056 passengers per hour per direction (pphpd). London's recently opened Crossrail (renamed fawningly at the eleventh hour as the Elizabeth line by former prime minister Boris Johnson) can currently only achieve 36,000 pphpd despite operating at GoA3. The limitation in both cases is the ability to safely get people from platform level to street level and vice versa.

The reason authorities are pursuing or at least attempting to pursue driverless technology for train operation is that there is a perception at a high level, particularly in government, that driverless trains will alleviate the pressures of a unionised workforce fighting for their pay and conditions; that driverless trains will avoid the disruption that strikes cause or — even more optimistically on their part — that driverless trains will do away with unionised staff altogether.

This is thankfully a false hope. Even on urban rail operations at GoA3 or GoA4, staff are required either on the trains or in a centralised control centre, and these staff can and will strike if their pay or conditions are under threat.

This isn't to say that driverless trains are an idea without merit. For example, driverless functionality can be used for train turnarounds to get the trains moving in the opposite direction faster than a driver can walk from one end to the other. Elements of driverless operation have been used for freight operations for many years with great success, particularly for slow loading or unloading of bulk goods or in container terminals.

And so we see again how railways provide us a lens through which to view developments and changes in other domains. These technologies can be harnessed usefully if they are matched with a real problem. It was the same with signalling; it was the same with mechanisation; it is the same with "autonomy".

There's no better example of tech being developed for its own sake than when autonomous transportation hits the road in the futile race to create viable driverless buses and cars. Nobody has been able to justify why driverless buses are a useful idea given the expense involved in trialling what will never functionally work. And driverless cars only make these efforts look more ridiculous — yet governments are fixated on a future where driverless cars ("autonomous vehicles") exist and require yet another era of reshaping our urban realm.

What problem are these technologies solving, other than justifying far higher sales costs per vehicle? Buses already have a highly complex and interactive system operating them (called drivers), and we already have autonomous vehicles — they are called taxis, and they exist basically everywhere.

Thankfully, driverless road vehicles will never functionally exist. Trials of driverless road tech date back to the 1950s if not earlier. Hardware has taken quantum leaps since then, yet we are no closer to seeing truly driverless vehicles on our roads. Even the current trials in the US significantly rely on low-paid workers in the global south ready to take control of the vehicle in conditions the computers don't like— and no amount of additional computing power, or point cloud resolution, or scanning frequency, or whatever, will solve these challenges. The wider context is that even if we did get closer, the more pressing issues of resource scarcity and climate collapse will distract us from just bunging more cash and attention at the automotive industry.

Conversely, driverless trains are really the latest, not particularly useful step in a long historic process of automating the control of trains and the wider railway systems on which they run and rely.

Large swathes of the tech industry claim to be fixated on a "move fast and break things" approach to innovation, but this is as wasteful for their sector as it is dangerous for safety-critical sectors like the railways, where a technology screw-up can risk lives if train-protection systems fail.

Fundamentally, technology must follow need, not lead it. Solutions must be people- and problem-led. Complicating our lives with greater reliance on unnecessary technology is a recipe for increasing costs, rising inequality and, as climate change bites harder, calamity.

This is as true for railways as it is for wider society. And we can test the success and viability of automation against two key measures that we'll explore next: the enabling of access to railway services, and the maintenance of the railways' complex system of systems.

# CHAPTER 2.7

# GETTING EVERYONE ONBOARD

Who should the railways be for?

Many railways and railway systems have been built — and continue to be built — to exclude rather than include large swathes of society. This is a condition we cannot repeat if railways are to solve our future mobility challenges. Whether on the grounds of disability, race, gender, social class or income group, there are plenty of examples of railways overcoming these challenges, but there are many more examples where selectiveness over who we serve remains prevalent. Discrimination remains common, not least considering the pressures of accessibility and affordability, and much of this is caused by the fact that those making decisions about railways generally come from a very small slice of society that is free from many of these pressures.

If we want the future to be better not just for some people but for everyone, then the railway that will deliver that future must be usable by everyone too.

To widen the range of people who can and will use railways as much as possible, we must understand the psychological and behavioural ways railways can drive modal shift towards sustainable transport, and maximise their deployment.

Broadly, there are six factors of human perception that railways harness either by default or by design in driving modal shift. This is very definitely true for urban systems such as trams or metros, but it equally applies to rural branch-line services and freight operations.

The six factors are: visibility, simplicity, integration, affordability, safety and ownership. I'll briefly go through each before drawing out the broader barriers to unlocking them.

Visibility is perhaps the most obvious benefit of railways. The permanence of the permanent way, if you like — there's no avoiding the fact that once tram tracks are laid or a station opens, it is there. Buses can come and go, routes can change, but the railway is unavoidably present.

This is true in the urban realm, but it also applies for rural areas, where the existence of a railway can put towns and villages on the map, even for people and businesses that may not actually use them. The presence of a rail freight interchange makes clear that it's an option for businesses to service their supply chain by rail.

Simplicity, rather than being something inherent to railway systems, is instead a virtue they must harness to maximise their usage. For passenger rail systems, the complexity of the network, ticketing, service patterns and indeed the design of stations and signage all have significant influence over people's desire to use them. For freight customers, anything other than the simplest possible access onto the railway is likely to push them into choosing road haulage without other disincentives being in place.

Integration for passengers requires that public transport systems be essentially agnostic about the technology they deploy. Transfers between lines should be free, and there should be no difference in fares whether you're on a tram, a metro, a commuter train, a bus, a funicular, a dangleway and so forth. Local routes should intersect or feed into high-capacity or longer-distance transport systems. Interchange stations should be just that, interchanges, and where different modes meet, their interchange stations should be integrated as well. Bus and train stations should be located in the same place!

Again, this is as critical for freight. Rail needs to be integrated into local distribution hubs, including cargo bike and electric van hubs. Rail also needs to integrate with road haulage hubs and, of course, harbours and ports. Interchange between modes has been accelerated, mostly for good, thanks to containerisation, but this only works if you've actually plugged the railway into the rest of your supply chain.

Integration also means ensuring that services are of a high-enough frequency to be useful for the people or goods that might be conveyed by them. More than any other factor, frequency is freedom. Coordinating connections is less complex if all services involved run at high frequencies.

Affordability is key — this does not necessarily mean cheapness, but it does mean that people and carriers need to perceive their journeys as being good value for money. A powerful way to convey value is through monthly or annual passes, such as Austria's Klimaticket, which enables travel across all public transport modes for €1,095 per year, or €3 a day.

Ticket prices are often used as a tool to manage demand, which is only a clever idea for public transport if you don't care about the future of the planet. In such instances, capacity is the limiting factor, and capacity ought to be improved to eradicate such practices.

Safety covers security and comfort, and this refers to the comfort of the journey as well as the comfort of travellers passing through vehicles and stations. It can refer also to the safety of goods being transported by rail.

This also refers to accessibility. If a traveller cannot use a system independently, they will choose another way.

Lastly, ownership is vital. This does not mean that a transport system needs to be state owned and administered (even if that is the right thing to do), but it does mean that people need to feel they have a collective stake in the branding, messaging and specification of services.

This feeds directly into questions of devolution, democratic oversight and the distance between decision-makers and decision-sufferers.

These six factors are not unique to railways. However, when combined with the fundamentals of energy and material efficiency, speed and capacity, it is these behavioural tricks that unlock the full potential of rail as a mass mover of people and things for short, medium and long distances.

## Form and function

I'm lucky to live in a city — old York, the original if perhaps not the best — that has a grand and once record-breaking railway station. The roof of the current station, built several decades after the first railway terminus was established in the city, is formed of several arches of increasing size, all swept in a curve to follow the line of the railway as it kinks its way from one company's straight railway to another company's straight railway running in the other direction.

Supported on almost one hundred columns, the wrought-iron ribs enclose an enormous space, including, originally, thirteen platforms — when it opened in 1877, York station was briefly the largest railway station in the world.

The experience of passengers at the time, even those used to the grand London termini, was one of awe. The scale of stations like the one in York impressed upon travellers not only that the railways were indelible and dominant, but that the town or city must have been worth their interest. On opening, the new station and the services it enabled permitted York's economy to thrive.

This remains absolutely true today. Form isn't secondary to function — it is intrinsic to it. Spaces that are impressive, appealing and spacious are also more capacious, comfortable and safe.

Not that this should be seen as a reason to lock station architecture into any given style. If York station was once the largest railway station in the world, it shows how rapidly the scale of the railways expanded from the late nineteenth century into the middle of the twentieth century. In 1906, the first stone was laid for what would become Europe's largest station by enclosed volume, and one that makes York look like a rural halt by comparison. It took nearly three decades, but Milan's Centrale station opened in 1931, an immense edifice of dizzying scale, tapping into a clumsy mixture of architectural styles. Successive changes to its design increased its grandeur, or rather the extent to which it sneered down on its future users. For me, this station is the perfect example of the sinister nature of architectural "traditionalists".

Architecture will always impose an ideology on the people who pass it, use it, work in it and live with it. In the case of Milan Centrale, to this day it makes passengers feel small, unworthy, daunted and insignificant to the power of the elite.

It is no coincidence, then, that this station was shaped and moulded as Italian fascism reached the height of its power. Mussolini himself wanted the station to carry forth the symbology of fascism, both literally (you can see where fasces and other fascist sculptural elements have been removed from the station's walls and columns, though plenty still remain) and experientially, with travellers arriving into the city being made to feel as close to insignificant as possible by the sheer volume of enclosed space crushing down onto their shoulders.

As an amateur architectural nerd myself, I find the station to be stylistically incoherent, not just because it is a mud pie of neoclassicism, art deco and art nouveau, but because of the cluttered nature and varying scales of its sculptural features. It is equally visually noisy and barren, and consequently not a hugely appealing space to navigate.

It is also difficult to ignore its more sinister features. An undercroft built with the original station was used to deport hundreds of Italian Jews to be murdered on an industrial scale during World War Two. At least one grand arrival room, thankfully inaccessible to the public, remains unchanged and retains swastikas in the tiled floor, intended specifically to welcome Adolf Hitler on his visits to the city.

For me, Milan Centrale is undeniably impressive, but it is also grotesque, and a terrific example of how we should never again build our stations. It isn't the only one, though.

If Milan Centrale was a statement piece embodying unlimited and intertwined capital and state power, then at the opposite end of the station design spectrum we can see what it looks like when the state is desperate to visibly if not practically retreat and leave capital unfettered and almighty. I can think of no better example than New York's Pennsylvania Station — Penn Station, as most know it.

Until the immense beaux-arts building above the platforms was demolished, Penn Station was a similarly grand edifice to Milan Centrale, with huge halls and staircases guiding passengers on an admittedly long-winded path from the street to their train. However, with a new chief executive joining as part of the enormous Penn Central railroad merger, the opportunity was taken to generate short-term cash, and the air rights were sold to the station site. Down came the head house, and the remaining sub-surface concourses were buried under a large steel platform while Madison Square Garden was erected above.

The original station was flawed, and its lack of preservation should not be considered a root cause of the current station's challenges. However, burying its original concourses and platforms under enormous over-site development with no view to its future has had precisely the outcome you'd expect. Today, with three times more passengers using the station than it was designed for, with long-distance services operated by Amtrak focused at Penn instead of Grand Central station, and with ever-increasing demand on its links to the other urban transport systems, the station complex is hopelessly inadequate, and expensive yet diminutive additions to it have failed to improve the experience for travellers.

It's a lesson hard learned, particularly in the Anglosphere. In the UK, it was bombs rather than outright neglect that put paid to the original and impressive station at Birmingham New Street. Yet, despite being owned by nationalised British Rail, the decision was still made to sell off the air rights of the station for development, boxing the platforms of the redeveloped station under concrete in such a way that the station became famous for its misery. A half-billion-pound investment in the station in the mid-2010s failed to resolve the poor conditions for passengers, in several ways making the station less rather than more accessible.

With this station still intact and still greatly disliked, the high-speed expansion of London Euston station intends to fully replicate these conditions, with a station site dominated by over-site development and the railway station elements relegated to the basement.

The inaccessibility of grand station termini cannot be ignored, either. Only since the turn of the century has Milan Centrale had escalators installed to enable passengers to avoid its enormous staircases. Penn station was originally built with only one escalator, despite a significant vertical gap between street and platform level. In Britain, the original London Euston, a station often cited as a great architectural loss, and (like Penn station) part responsible for a second wave of architectural preservation in the UK, was in fact a hodgepodge of various buildings, including a great hall that relied on grand and inaccessible staircases.

At a time of great optimism for the future, slightly before the car had edged its way into a position of total dominance in the minds of policymakers, this cluttered mess was swept away to be replaced by a clean, open, modern and accessible station, built with the passenger's needs front and centre. However, today's Euston has become a victim of its own success, with the station hopelessly ill-equipped for the enormous number of passengers now relying on it, and with retail provision encroaching on a now too small concourse.

There's more to accessibility than escalators and clear walking routes, though. As a station I've used a lot, the changes made to Birmingham New Street as part of its mid-2010s makeover typifies poor decision-making and late-stage changes to design that result in a very unappealing station to navigate.

The use of bands of darker and lighter tiling make it look like there are stairs on the shallow ramps required to access the concourse from street level, an acknowledged accessibility challenge. Handrails are located in the middle rather than at the edge of walkways, meaning you have to cross the flow of people to reach them. Low levels of lighting on the approaches to the concourse are further compounded by an open ceiling broken up with curved cosmetic panels, providing an assault on the eyes that can be discombobulating for anyone with partial sight or prone to sensory overload.

Even if you don't mind any of that, escalators to the mezzanine level (where you can grab a burrito and get your nails done) are not positioned opposite the departure boards so that you can read which platform you need to run to, but are oriented so that you have to cross the concourse before being able to read them. Once you've managed this, you then have to work out how the hell to navigate a bizarre labyrinth of glass dividers, barricades of ticket gates and myriad colour-labelled waiting areas to finally slip down to your platform and choke on diesel fumes.

Perhaps the most embarrassing mistake made following the partial reversal of the burying of the station in the 1960s sits high above your head. A new roof was built spanning the concourse to bring in some natural light as part of the refurbishment works, and while it is architecturally innocuous, it uses a material more commonly employed in large greenhouses. Without the open ends usually associated with railway station train sheds, the sealed environment has had exactly the effect you might imagine: even a moderate bit of sunlight results in temperatures climbing rapidly on the concourse, melting the confectionary in the Pret A Manger and — perhaps more egregiously — boiling its occupants alive. Not a forward-thinking move as a changing climate brings us hotter and hotter days for more of the year.

Throwing money at a landmark architect and giving them free reign is also not the answer. Nobody embodies this better than the architectural antics of Santiago Calatrava.

It is difficult to argue that his stations aren't stunning, and indeed most of them are successful, particularly when integrated well into the wider urban environment, such as at Gare do Oriente, where the former embankment gave way to a far more permeable structure, removing a linear barrier between the waterfront and inland elements of Lisbon's Parque das Nações.

However, Gare do Oriente also gives us examples of where the singular vision of one architect can get in the way of the function of a station. Calatrava made little allowance for kiosks or other retail amenities within his station, with these having to be added as later afterthoughts and only at the protestation of the architect. Similarly, few or no benches were included in areas of congregation, an unpleasantly emerging theme for new or renovated station concourses. The famous "forest of steel" platform canopies at Gare do Oriente are designed in such a way that they offer scant protection from the elements. In all, you get the feeling that this station and others that Calatrava has created are focused too much on the architect's vision and too little on the widespread and diverse needs of staff and passengers.

You might be thinking, "So what do you think is a good station?" given I've dismissed grand neoclassical heaps, underground bunkers and landmark sculptural creations. Well, the reality is that it isn't particularly the typology of these stations that I have a problem with; it's who these stations have been built for that causes the problems. Milan Centrale was built for the fascist elite to make its users feel insignificant. Passengers were, at best, an afterthought when Pennsylvania Station was flattened and the concourses were buried under a stadium. Calatrava's stations are increasingly built for the vanity of the architect and the politicians commissioning him.

To succeed, stations must be built for those who will use them. Today's and tomorrow's passengers must be front and centre in the minds of those developing new or upgraded stations, but so too must be those who will build, operate and maintain them. It may sound trite, but it is critical that these people are in the room when pen is first put to paper on any station project.

Accessibility needs are diverse, and as such cannot be achieved by adherence to standards alone — the complexity of stations, even small ones, means you need to consult with the people whose needs must be met by them. The best way to do this is by bringing together independent experts with personal and professional experience in building inclusive spaces and facilities. Such panels exist for railways across the world, and in Britain this role is carried out by Network Rail's Built Environment Accessibility Panel. Their work is vital and leaves a better railway for everyone.

Naturally, most stations are not enormous multi-platform termini dominating dense city centres. At the opposite end of the scale are the little stations, and their role is equally important. These places represent a focal point for movement in a given locality, and accordingly can and should represent it. Railways can and do draw a line through communities, and as much effort as possible should be made in their design to mitigate this and tie those communities back together.

Little stations provide that opportunity, creating a crossing point in the railway that draws people through it. Therefore, they can act as local hubs, not just for passengers, but for everyone that passes through them. These stations should be crafted with the same care that the big stations are — function and form should not just be defined by the technical specifications and the budget.

Such stations should also be the hub for local transport, just as large stations act as a focal point for urban transport systems. Large car parks may have their role today, but long-term aspirations for stations should move away from the parkway model in favour of the prioritisation of sustainable modes, not least walking, wheeling and cycling.

Stations are a classic example of liminal spaces — that is, environments where people transition between their start location and the journey, or between their journey and their destination. As such, people involuntarily spend a lot of time in these spaces, and attention to the quality of that experience should be key.

There's a term that gets thrown around a lot, "destination stations", that refers to the intent of passengers to dwell at railway stations not because their train has been delayed, but because the station has some innate appeal or draw that makes them attractive places to visit in their own right.

Unfortunately, in the majority of cases this refers not to the amenity or architectural merit of the station, but rather its retail offering. I'm a fan of rapid-fire baked goods as much as the next Scotsman, but the value of station spaces goes far beyond extracting the maximum business rates from retail tenants.

There are two features that stations should embody above all else, and this applies to the bigger story that the railway is telling as well. Those are permeability and purpose.

Firstly, the most important thing railways can provide travellers is time.

In an increasingly busy world, with minds occupied by ever-more-complex interactions throughout our working and non-working lives, the least the railways can do is steal as little time from people as possible, allowing them more time with friends and family and to enjoy company, culture, competition and humanity's general creative endeavour. This is key for driving modal shift, too. In most environments, the railways are competing with the convenience of stepping out of your house and into your car.

This means that navigation in the station space is key. It must be well signed and uncluttered; both horizontal and vertical navigation must be quick, easy and intuitive. This all maximises the station's permeability.

But stations must also be purposeful. They are, first and foremost, transport hubs, and so the ability to access transport services in and out of the station must be paramount. Everything else is secondary.

For an immensely complex system of systems, the interface with the user is necessarily challenging to get right. This is true of stations, but it is also true of train information before and during the journey, and of how users buy their tickets. It is absolutely also true for the transportation of goods, when working out how to convey your goods by rail is likely to be further down the list than "who on earth do I contact to even begin to work out if this is feasible?"

Indeed, if you step back, you can start to see that an effective framework for developing the ideal railway station is also applicable to any interface of public services and the people using them. Simplicity is key, but so too is the lasting impression left on the user. You want the interface, no matter what it is intended to facilitate, to be both permeable (people can get through that interface quickly, easily and at volume) and purposeful (there's no need for any extraneous processes or information).

This doesn't preclude attractiveness being built in; indeed, it is likely that an attractive system will be a functional one, as it will achieve both permeability and purpose. We should not shy away from our public buildings and spaces being beautiful — art and cultural engagement bring joy and meaning to life, and contribute to the permanence of systems. We can and should have nice things, but beauty has many secondary benefits.

Most fundamental, of course, is that no matter what the architectural quality of the railway station, the clarity of the online timetable or the intuitiveness of the ticket machine, if the underlying system is not functional, the user is going to be rightly dissatisfied.

When London Euston's reconstruction was completed, a regularised timetable of fast, electric, air-conditioned trains provided a world-leading rail service up and down the West Coast Main Line towards Birmingham, Liverpool, Manchester and Glasgow. The new station (and others along the line) was a critical component in providing this modern experience, but without the railway service it would have been for nought.

## Level boarding or death

One might assume that allowing all travellers to access trains independently and safely would be the first priority of any passenger railway system, but across the world, this isn't the case.

There are all sorts of reasons why, but I'd argue the most important and complex element of fully accessible provision is the interface between the train and the platform. It isn't particularly challenging from an engineering perspective, but it represents the interaction between multiple levels of government, between management authorities, between owners, operators and manufacturers of trains, and between those who own, maintain and expand rail infrastructure. That makes optimising this interface very challenging.

The earliest passenger rail vehicles were generally adapted from stagecoach bodies and were accessed from ground level in much the same way as stagecoaches had been for the preceding century. As the modern railway system emerged in the second quarter of the nineteenth century, the idea of a raised platform to meet the carriage emerged. However, this was little higher than a step or two — the idea of providing level access was a long way off.

By the 1860s, rail vehicle design had moved on, but the PTI had seen little improvement. Indeed, in 1865 the Franklin Institute reported on "the frequent loss of life that occurred at station platforms, from persons getting in or out of carriages", and stated in no uncertain terms that "platforms should be built up to the level of the flooring of the carriages, and that a dangerous space between the platform and the carriages ought not to exist".

The response of the railway companies at the time is a familiar one to campaigners for level boarding today: "It must be remembered that railways were not the system of a day." In other words, the legacy of different platform heights that the ever-amalgamating railway companies inherited made it expensive to resolve the differences in platform heights and rolling stock floor heights. This excuse still gets rolled out by contemporary railway authorities, despite countries like the UK having had unified national systems for many decades. But this isn't the only common challenge.

While so-called level-boarding systems have been in operation for decades across the globe, these are most commonly on dedicated, segregated suburban systems such as metros or trams. Achieving level boarding on mixed-traffic railways is more complex, owing to the need to accommodate various cross-sectional train dimensions, including freight trains and long-distance trains. Indeed, London's Elizabeth line offers a lesson in flawed decision-making on this front, as platforms in the expansive city centre underground stations have been set to match the higher-floored trains, despite those trains calling at mixed traffic platforms outside of the urban core set to the national standard. This means that this brand-new railway has cornered itself into perpetually operating an inaccessible service, as new trains will always have to deal with two different platform heights.

Nevertheless, for the incumbent train manufacturers, the cost of completely redesigning the sub- and superstructure of a train body, which in the case of the most common train fleet family in Britain have been essentially unchanged since the 1980s, makes adapting trains to match the standard platform height an unpopular choice.

This has opened the door to outsiders, and with their extensive experience of providing level boarding on mixed fleets in Switzerland in particular, non-incumbent manufacturers (from a UK perspective) have seen a gap in the market and pounced on it, providing so-called low-floored trains that match Britain's standard platform position.

Low-floor rural, urban and long-distance trains are now operating services across Britain, and have proved incredibly popular, to the point that train operators and devolved authorities are pressing for level boarding to become the standard provision for new train fleets.

The PTI must be thought of as a system, though, and while procuring low-floored trains is a significant leap forwards, full level boarding cannot be achieved without all platforms being set to the national standard offsets.

While many station platforms have been built or corrected to match the standard platform position, a far greater number remain outside of these tolerances. Of these, plenty are small stations where minimal effort would be required for corrective works. However, most stations would require additional work to station buildings, track layouts, bridges, lift thresholds, platform drainage and so on, resulting in platform correction works being complex and costly.

No matter what level of government leads on delivering this work, the benefits of level boarding are inescapable and multi-fold. Providing a nearly gap-free PTI improves safety, accessibility and dwell times. In Britain, incidents at the PTI account for the greatest number of passenger fatalities and injuries on the railway, and is the only risk to passengers getting worse, not better. Bluntly, it isn't credible for a railway authority to say that safety is its number-one priority while committing little or no resources to achieving level boarding and reducing the harm caused at the PTI.

Meanwhile, the exclusion of an ageing population from independent travel by rail is clearly untenable, particularly as elderly, disabled and otherwise vulnerable people often have less access to private transport alternatives. People who use wheelchairs, families with buggies, tourists with luggage — there isn't a single passenger who doesn't benefit from level boarding.

While the political challenges far outweigh the engineering challenges, achieving level boarding should be a core aim of any railway system, either rural, urban, regional or high-speed. If the economics don't stack up, the calculations to determine them aren't configured correctly. This really gets to the heart of the reason railways currently limit the number and type of people who can access them. As long as the authorities that distribute funds to railways see the return from that funding only in narrow terms, nothing will ever be fixed.

Making these changes does not require revolution, but it does require incredibly deep and fundamental changes to the way that governments view economic success. The railways, like any public service, do not and cannot exist in a bubble, and to be fully unleashed, government needs to be incentivised not to create an economy of individual prosperity, but one of collective prosperity.

## Fair fares

The dominance of an economic system that by its nature requires winners and losers — rewarding those who already have wealth and power at the expense of most other folk — means that disabled people are only one group in a large pool of people denied access to the shared wealth of our species, not just in terms of money, land or resources, but in knowledge and culture.

For railways in much of the world, fares are used to manage demand in lieu of expanding system capacity. This only makes sense on a short-term basis to limit the risk of unsafe overcrowding, but in the longer term, demand should always be satisfied to achieve the maximum modal shift to rail.

It isn't just the absolute cost of fares that prevents people from using rail, but the variety or quality of ticketing websites, the non-existence of station booking facilities and — crucially — the perceived complexity of ticketing systems.

It may drive commercial value in the short term, but dynamic ticketing does not generally create the perception of affordability. It may be true that, two months in advance, you can find cheap tickets, but that's no good to most travellers, who don't plan their lives that far ahead. The result is that those who can afford higher prices often travel on the cheapest tickets, and those who would benefit from cheaper tickets cannot make the most of them. The perception of affordability would be enhanced in this instance by getting rid of the cheapest tickets but bringing turn-up-and-go ticket prices down as well.

Ticket offers or discounts that rely on up-front purchases exclude those without access to more than a week's worth of income. Railcards, commonly used on the British rail network, should be abolished and fares simply reduced to match for all passengers. The German €49 go-anywhere ticket, the Austrian Klimaticket, season tickets — all of these require significant sums of money, meaning that only the rich can afford the cheapest tickets. It's backwards. This doesn't mean that these passes are not good — they should be offered with options for spreading the cost, or for free as part of the social security that supports those least well off in society.

Further simplification can be achieved by removing peak fares, applying zonal fares systems for devolved railway networks and providing contactless ticketing (so long as cash-based tickets or free travelcards are available for those without means).

The last question to tackle is whether public transport fares should be gotten rid of altogether. This is a rare question for which I do not have a confident answer. The evidence of the success of free public transport in driving increased modal share, at least in the medium term, is mixed. However, as the modal share increases and railways become the backbone of travel, the balance of fare versus subsidy may shift. The complete removal of fares would bring with it an immense reduction in administrative complexity and costs, train and station staff workload and station clutter, and a great improvement in the ease of travel for all.

However, fares are only part of the picture of making rail as widely popular as possible. Research has shown that cheap fares can just result in existing rail users travelling more, rather than widening out the pool of passengers. We see, therefore, that understanding the barriers to rail usage beyond cost are critical for making rail the first choice for as many people as possible.

## Diversity is vital

To achieve everything we've talked about already, it isn't just the spatial or temporal scope of decision-making that needs to change; we also need to diversify the people making those decisions. The same people have been making the decisions that shape our society for several decades, while the pace of development has slowed and many of our material conditions have worsened, so it is clear that the homogeneity of those decision-makers is hampering our ability to achieve change. This includes greater representation of race and of indigenous populations who, across the globe, are suffering some of the most significant impacts of our changing climate — and of our responses to it.

Complex challenges demand diversity of thought, and diversity of thought demands diversity of experience. Making decisions and solving these enormous, interconnected problems also requires everyone to be able to live as their true selves. Invariably, the problems we've discussed already fall hardest on the shoulders of women. Empowering them to move around as freely as possible is a key component in giving women equity — allowing them to live their lives independently and giving them access to reproductive services and safety from male violence. As the USA rolls back its protections of women and LGBTQ+ people, public transport is a key means for lower income women and trans people to move from hostile to haven states. Many women do not have access to a car, particularly those in non-white communities. Both bus and rail have a role to play, but between states, rail ought to play a far bigger role.

Why is this all pertinent to shaping our future railway system, though?

Our existing railway systems are inaccessible because people disabled by those systems haven't been involved in developing them. Fares are used to limit demand because policymakers have not experienced transport poverty and the ill effects of a car-dominant society.

If the railways are to carry a greater slice of the population around, then they have a greater responsibility to champion diversity, indeed to celebrate the diversity of their staff. As an industry but also as a public amenity, the railways cannot adequately serve society and all of its needs without themselves being representatively diverse.

# CHAPTER 2.8

# SURVIVING THE FUTURE

It's all very well saying that the railways will fix the future, but to do so they also must be able to survive the future.

Of the challenges society faces today and tomorrow, many present direct threats to the future operation of the railways. Global heating, the changing climate and the weather effects it creates are certainly the biggest, but our increasing use of connective technologies exposes the railway to cyber-attacks. Corporate interests will be an increasing threat, too, and tackling them may require unusual tricks.

Beyond climate change, humanity's challenges can be thought of in terms of the timescale on which they are acting. Some challenges are manifesting now and require an immediate response. Others are developing over a longer period and require longer-term action. If thinking about these timescales helps us understand the speed and shape of any response, categorising these challenges as short-term and long-term can help governments at all levels develop and prioritise responses to them.

We've already talked about the shortage of skilled people as an existential threat to the future of the railways, and we've considered in detail how we resolve it, but as we move deeper into the twenty-first century, the scarcity of material resources will play a bigger part in how we develop and deliver railway systems.

By handing greater control of railways to the people who use them, the political risk of any positive change being reversed can be mitigated, but assuming we can make these changes, incumbent political and corporate powers will perhaps be the most difficult obstacles to overcome.

## Getting battered by the climate

Much as there is far more talk of climate change today versus when I was born, the reality is that there has been remarkably little action to back up those words. Only in 2016 did the Paris Agreement commit the world to holding global warming at around 1.5 °C, while 2023 saw the global average temperature anomaly reach... 1.5 °C. It was the warmest year on record.

A few degrees Celsius may not sound like much when averaged across the planet, but accepting that there are thousands if not millions of pages of scientific exposition you can dive into to understand the details, let me deploy my rather hack analogy that I use when I'm explaining the relationship between climate and weather to students.

I've always been a fan of Lava Lamps, with their somewhat mesmerising blobbing making up for their hopelessness at lighting a room. With the heating element set at its lowest, the masses of dyed fluid rise and fall predictably and gently. Our planet's weather systems are largely driven by movements of large air masses of varying temperature and moisture content. In our Lava Lamp, as we turn up the dial on the heating element, which varies the temperature only by a few degrees, the movement of the blobs becomes more rapid and unpredictable. At a certain temperature we see that there's a tipping point — the blobs no longer follow any pattern of movement, breaking apart and bouncing off each other without any predictability whatsoever.

As our climate warms, the same behaviour we see of our Lava Lamp blobs is mirrored by the air masses and atmospheric cells that drive our weather. Even a slight increase in temperature results in greatly increased drama and unpredictability. Weather systems become more erratic, extremes more common. It has been called "global weirding" and it doesn't gel well with the way humans have developed our civilisation on this funny little rock hurtling through space.

And that's on top of the steadier changes global warming heating will bring to seasonal temperatures, precipitation, sea levels, and the rest.

Dr Alex Priestley, a meteorologist and geophysicist, explains the context for the United Kingdom:

> As global temperatures increase, the UK will see more weather extremes. Heatwaves and summer droughts are getting much more likely, as is heavy rainfall and high winds. This means more inland flooding. As sea levels rise, we'll see more coastal flooding too.

Heat isn't the only consequence of global warming, but it is one of the most widespread, and its impacts for running a transport system — particularly a railway — can be both chronic and acute. Understanding how to respond to them, and how to tackle any secondary effects of this response, can therefore be instructive for us in understanding how to build a society that can survive climate change.

A lack of effective (or any) air conditioning on trains is probably the number one problem for today's railways. Even where trains do have air conditioning, only the newest trains have systems that are rated to bring internal temperatures down to a comfortable level in extreme heat. Trains much more than a decade old will often have air conditioning that can barely provide any cooling at all when the external temperature exceeds 30 °C.

This makes conditions for passengers and particularly staff — who have to spend all day in overheated trains — absolutely intolerable. Things are no better for station staff on platforms or in offices and control rooms without sufficient air conditioning.

Trains themselves start having issues in extreme heat too, with traction systems, electronics and even brakes overheating, in some cases to the extent that trains have to stop or won't start.

Infrastructure problems certainly have a major impact, though — there are many issues that designers attempt to alleviate and maintainers must tackle when things get hot. Track buckling resulting from the unrestrained thermal expansion of steel rails is probably the most well known. As a rule of thumb, rails get twenty degrees hotter than the surrounding air temperature. In Britain, the highest-quality track has what's called a "critical rail temperature" (that is, a "take action" temperature) of 59 °C. Add twenty degrees to the UK's now broken temperature record of 40 °C and you can see why this is a problem.

Older designs of overhead electrification equipment can sag as contact and catenary wires expand in the heat, which in turn increases the risk of a train's pantograph pulling them down. Even newer, auto-tensioning systems have a limiting design temperature. When (not if) countries see those limiting temperatures being regularly exceeded, those systems will be outside of their design capability.

Signalling systems that control trains very rarely rely on cables or bars that expand in the heat anymore, but lineside equipment can still overheat. As train and traffic control systems are increasingly digitised, server operating temperatures become a critical issue, and shutdowns are necessary in extreme heat to avoid permanent damage, potentially knocking out the railways of whole regions.

Sustained or even short periods of high temperatures can also desiccate and shrink earthworks, resulting in rough rides, and sometimes in sufficiently deformed track that a line needs to close. Though these are generally longer-term problems to deal with, they add pressure to an already over-stressed asset. In addition, extremes of rainfall caused by the higher moisture-carrying capacity of warm air can overwhelm drainage systems, including those built to the latest standards, which in turn can lead to railways being washed out. Lineside fires from dry vegetation and — in extreme conditions — overcooked track or lineside components are also a genuine and serious threat.

The ability of staff to safely get out to monitor high-risk areas or to respond to failures will also be severely impacted, which in turn impacts on the ability to run trains at speed or at all.

Heat is a potentially lethal issue everywhere, and in many cases the impacts and mitigations are more substantial than in the UK. However, for the railways and built environment more broadly, extreme heat is not the most significant challenge, even if its impact is more widespread.

As extremes of drought and rainfall have become more frequent and pronounced, the ground on which the railway sits is also being pushed to its limits. Network Rail (Britain's state-owned infrastructure owner) manages around 16,000 route-km, of which 60% utilises earthworks — that's 10,000 km of embankments and cuttings to keep intact.

On average, there are around one hundred earthworks failures every year that result in an impact on train services in Great Britain, though this average has fluctuated over the last few years, reaching as high as 140 per year. Ten years ago, this figure was only at sixty-five failures annually.

A substantially busier railway means that even if trains are only indirectly impacted through delays, these quickly ripple around the network causing major problems such as displaced staff and overcrowding. Even more critically, more services means an increased risk of a train being derailed by an earthworks failure — and the consequences of this can be severe, not least if more than one train is involved.

On the morning of 12 August 2020, a thankfully quiet express train (this was the middle of the pandemic) rounded a curve near Carmont in northeast Scotland and struck a heaped mass of stones and rubble. The wheels of the train were lifted off the rails, and as the curve reversed in the other direction, the train's forward momentum took it over the edge of a bridge and into the embankment on the other side.

The crash resulted in the deaths of the driver, a guard and a passenger. The remaining six people aboard were all injured. Had the train been as full as usual, the death toll would have been far higher.

That morning, a severe storm had swept across Scotland and the northeast in particular. Infrastructure failures from flooding and washouts were popping up faster than the control room overseeing Scotland's railways could comprehend, and the team lost situational awareness. Meanwhile, the extreme rainfall had already disrupted the train that would later derail, as it had been stopped by a flood further down the line. Without additional instruction from the centralised controllers, and with the weather having visibly improved, the stuck train returned northwards at full speed. Up the line, an extremely localised pocket of very heavy rain dropped a deluge on a section of the railway adjacent to a single-sided cutting.

Railway accidents only ever occur when a series of circumstances align, and the Carmont derailment is no different.

At the crest of the cutting was a drain that ran downhill, and for reasons that have been lost to time, the contractor who built the drain had ignored the design, half-built one section and invented their own solution for another, which on the day of the accident channelled a deluge of water into the poorly built section, washing it out onto the tracks.

Had the designer and client organisations fulfilled their obligations, the accident would have been avoided. Had the drain actually been added to the asset register and been inspected fully, the accident would have been avoided. Yet the localised cloudburst washed out the drainage system, which in turn derailed the train.

All these separate, overlapping issues led to the first fatal main-line derailment in the UK since 2007. And each of the contributing factors will become more prevalent as railways move into the future, either due to climate change or pressures to deliver a more intensive service using existing tracks and trains.

It's an extreme example, but it is also a lesson in everything that can and will go wrong without due care for the health of the railway and its operating procedures. Climate change isn't just a threat to resilient operations — it will eventually represent the biggest threat to the safety of railway operations.

## Embedding resilience

So what are the solutions? Let's think about heat first.

Steel rails can only really operate in an extreme window of about ninety degrees — the only control engineers like me have is to choose where that range sits (e.g., from -30 °C to 60 °C, as is the case in mainland Europe). The question this presents infrastructure managers and their engineers is: Do we account for higher temperatures and cope with more rail breaks in winter, or do we minimise rail breaks and run a reduced service on an increasing number of summer days?

Many countries have to restress (the process of stretching and welding rails to resist compressive thermal forces) their tracks twice a year, which is enormously costly and disruptive — on any densely used network, this is simply not feasible. Italy paints almost all of their rails white, but again this is costly and has limited effectiveness when extremely high temperatures are becoming more common. Sliding the operational temperature window of rails upwards can keep tracks safer in the heat, but this increases the likelihood of more rail breaks in winter. And climate change potentially means we'll see more extremes in both directions.

Countries like the Netherlands spend enough money on infrastructure renewals that almost no older, less-resilient track remains in regular operation, greatly reducing the need for restrictions. This is an effective way to get the most out of the available operating range of steel rails, and it requires the political commitment to the future that most Anglospheric economies lack.

By building new railway lines, engineers can design out many of the failure modes I've listed, for example by using slab track (which is essentially buckle-proof up to much higher temperatures) and by minimising lineside equipment. Running only newer trains with capable air conditioning is another way to keep passengers and staff safe and cool — the newest fleets can generally cope in the more extreme heat.

The task gets harder year on year, though. Network Rail is dealing with an array of challenges: decades of bare-minimum patch-and-mend, the tremendous leap in traffic that the railway is carrying, and the increases in extremes of wet and dry. This is compounded by recent, government-instigated cuts to its frontline maintenance workforce, and the mothballing of some of its fleet of on-track renewals machines.

In hot weather, the age and condition of infrastructure is the key metric by which a decision is made about where closures or speed restrictions must occur. Where air temperatures reach or exceed the upper thresholds of operation, even the newest track and overhead line equipment (OLE) isn't designed to operate normally. Where older systems exist, such as "unstressed" switches and crossings or fixed-tension OLE, this means widespread speed restrictions or closures.

Slowing down trains is an effective way to keep some form of service running — track buckles are a dynamic phenomenon and occur under trains, so slowing trains down reduces the likelihood of a buckle while also reducing the consequences should one occur. For OLE, the same is true for sagging overhead wires. Slower trains are less likely to cause a dewirement and make less mess even if they do pull the wires down.

Ultimately, short of relying more heavily on closures and speed restrictions, the volume of maintenance and renewals must rise. We cannot say we are doing as much as we can while decades-old junction layouts remain in place, or whilst the maintenance of track stress and ballast profiles (both critical in avoiding buckles) falls behind.

It cannot be the case that, as the number of extreme weather days increases, so too does the number of days the railway throws up its arms and says, "No trains today." If we are to drive modal shift away from road and air, then rail needs to be our most capable transport system. And its fundamentals — fixed guideways, fail-safe control systems, trained staff — mean it is by far the most suitable mode of transport to rely on during climate extremes.

However, the grim reality is that engineers the world over aren't keeping up, and given the pressures of a diminishing pool of skilled staff and ever-decreasing windows of access onto the railways to maintain or repair them, we have to do things differently.

How, then, can new ideas help to reduce the likelihood and impacts of climate change? How can meaningful innovation bolster rail's resilience to ensure it keeps people and goods moving as countries endure weather extremes?

There are technological innovations that can allow us to tinker around the edges of the problem, such as under-sleeper pads that can extend ballast life, or water-attenuation technologies that minimise the need for new infrastructure while protecting what is already in place.

We've already talked about the role of automation throughout the railway's history; the latest revolution is the collection, processing and — crucially — analysis of potentially limitless volumes of data about asset condition of trains and infrastructure. Data collection of this sort is nothing new, but where the opportunity lies is in the scale of the data that automated and high-resolution inspection techniques offer, combined with the ability to harness machine and deep learning to interrogate the data alongside other metrics such as weather data.

Railways are getting older. They are getting more heavily used. There is less time to access them for inspection or maintenance. They are getting battered by a rapidly changing climate. At the moment, engineers are losing the battle. Harnessing mass asset data is the key to winning the war.

Let's quickly look at some examples.

A comprehensive network of rail sensors can allow a much more accurate picture of rail temperatures to be built up remotely, which helps asset engineers guide maintainers to risk spots and can also allow a more targeted approach to speed restrictions, minimising disruption. Analysing the relationship between measured air temperatures, solar flux and rail temperatures can then allow forecasted predictions of when and where appropriate measures can be deployed — or even where the design of the railway can tackle high rail temperatures in the first place.

Physical remote monitoring is one way in which we have been better predicting the condition of earthworks, preventing sudden failures and avoiding the danger and disruption they cause. This can be via sensors on or near tracks, via dedicated or even in-service on-train equipment, or using drones and satellites. Again, the immediate data related to earthwork health is only one small part of the picture — enabling a better understanding of the whole network and its response to weather conditions allows longer-term predictions to be made about design and operation.

In Britain, rebuilding the entire railway's drainage system probably wouldn't be a bad idea, but engineers would never get enough access to the railway to dig it all up. Instead, observed and predicted weather data, modelling of wider flood catchments and the analysis of track quality and use of non-destructive inspection techniques can enable an understanding of what drainage exists and is fit for purpose, and what is likely to give up the ghost at the next deluge.

For such innovations to make a difference, railway authorities need to be supported to fund such developments on an ongoing basis, and to store, manage and make the most of the resulting data. Where railways do not have their own well-developed research and development function, universities can bolster and enhance this capability.

Equally as important is that improved weather and climate forecasting supports clearer operational and strategic thinking. While this is very much the domain of meteorological modellers such as the Met Office, Deutscher Wetterdienst and NASA's Global Modeling and Assimilation Office, there should be a closer working partnership with railway authorities to match their needs and provide insights into their infrastructure data. Such collaboration could unlock far more accurate and useful insights into the behaviour of railway assets under various forecasted weather conditions, allowing changes to railway design or to planned responses to weather events.

Automation and the use of data to accelerate the diagnosis of problems and possible solutions present enormous opportunities, but as we discussed in the previous chapter, they bring their own challenges.

Politicians and operating authorities can see technology as a justification for cutting funding and frontline roles. Technology itself, not least the sensors and other monitoring systems, is vulnerable to heat and moisture. The nature of the market for these tools lends itself to the proliferation of proprietary hard- and software, with all the problems that causes, not least obsolescence over the lifespan of the asset. If a startup tech provider of a remote monitoring widget folds, which is a pretty likely outcome, then what happens to the kit they've deployed. Who pays for its replacement?

There are no perfect answers to these questions (well-funded and empowered asset owners are clearly vital), but unless we make the most of the data revolution, when it comes to the impact of a changing climate on our railway, the challenge might be insurmountable. The Carmont derailment realised the British rail industry's worst fears: that its infrastructure is being pushed harder than its engineers can keep pace with.

As with so many aspects of our ageing, bombarded rail system, a rapid deployment of technology provides an opportunity, not to cut budgets or headcounts, but to allow us to do much more, much quicker. Those key resources we have — skilled people, track access, machines and time, among others — can be better deployed if we can harness data collection, analysis and interpretation effectively.

The reality is that we don't have a choice. For most of the world, winters are only going to get wetter, and summers are only going to get hotter.

## Hijacking the railway

However, in hooking up more and more rail assets — trains, infrastructure, etc. — to externally accessible networks, we open up the whole system to another future threat, or rather an existing threat that is only growing as time passes.

In October 2022, two acts of what appeared to be targeted vandalism managed to bring all trains in northern Germany to a halt for three hours, with consequent disruption lasting much longer. Officials described the incident as "a targeted and professional attack on the railroads".[5]

In an age when information is more easily accessible than at any time in history, malicious actors can gain an understanding of critical systems from their mobile device with a few taps of the thumb. In the case of the 2022 attack, two separate sites at opposite ends of Deutsche Bahn's network had seen telecoms cables cut in a manner which maximised the impact on the operational railway.

---

[5] Josefine Fokuhl (2022) "Attack on German Rail Network 'Targeted, Professional,' Police Say", *Bloomberg*, 9 October, available online from: https://www.bloomberg.com/news/articles/2022-10-09/attack-on-german-rail-network-targeted-professional-police

Physical attacks on networked systems are less common, but virtual attacks are becoming routine for public service providers across the globe. The railway is no exception. In July 2021, a ransomware attack — in which a system is locked such that it is inaccessible to users — shut down brand-new ticketing machines in stations across the north of England for over a week. Rogue updates to virus software have resulted in the computers of infrastructure managers being locked out under similar circumstances.

As our railway systems become more complex, more interconnected and more centralised, and as they rely more heavily on sending information via IP (internet protocol) networks, they also become more exposed to targeted attacks, whereby only the slightest physical intrusion (or an attack conducted without any physical interaction at all) can bring hundreds or even thousands of trains to a halt (or worse, into each other's paths).

Does this mean that we should return everything to the days of mechanical interlocking, points rodding and box-per-block signalling? Of course not. It does, however, mean that practitioners of infrastructure design need to be more than cursorily aware of the opportunities for attacks like these as we plug more assets into the "internet of things". It also means we need to assimilate more expertise from outside of the railway industry.

Only by matching railway expertise with security expertise can we minimise the threat of these sorts of incidents. People with "traditional" railway knowledge need the support of experts in fields such as cyber security, just as the cyber security people we bring into the industry need to understand how the decisions they make impact the way the railway operates.

How, then, does the specification of new or modified infrastructure take account of these threats? How do we facilitate the two camps of expertise to work together to ensure railway operations don't compromise security and security doesn't compromise railway operations?

To make railways as safe and reliable as possible given the much more intensive type of operations seen today compared with one hundred years ago, they rely on a complex array of connected systems using the same IP network. On Britain's railways, this system is called the fixed telephone network (FTNx), and installation of the original version of this system began nearly two decades ago.

Across the British network, train control, command and communication systems (telecoms and signalling) increasingly rely on FTNx. Conventional signalling systems installed recently — as well as the new digital signalling systems being rolled-out Europe-wide — use networked systems to relay information to and from rail operating centres. This covers the location of trains, the activation of lineside and in-cab signals, the operation of points, lineside telephones and so on.

Signalling and telecoms are only one element of networked railway control, too. Traction power and distribution systems (the infrastructure that powers trains) also uses FTNx to enable operation of electrification from virtual electrical control rooms integrated into the rail operating centres, unifying train control and traction control under one roof. This approach continues to be rolled out to legacy electrification systems, but new systems incorporate SCADA — supervisory control and data acquisition, the system that controls traction power and distribution — by default.

The increasingly ungainly pile of use-cases for interconnected systems doesn't stop there. Remote condition monitoring of assets, CCTV, passenger and freight customer information systems, even lighting controls can all be pinned into IP networks. And fixed-IP networks are only one part of the puzzle.

GSM-R radio provides a dedicated connection between signallers and drivers, and enables an alternative communication path between trains, lineside assets and traffic control systems as the digital railway rolls out. It provides another route for all of the secondary applications mentioned above.

Even the public mobile communications network is used for transmitting information seen as not being safety-critical, including data for on-train Wi-Fi and on-demand video or yet more remote condition monitoring. The number of SIM cards clipped into widgets glued onto bits of railway is increasing exponentially.

With this enormous pile of different communication systems and use-cases comes the key question: How on earth do we guarantee the security of the railway?

Just as safety is embedded throughout the design process, security must also be embedded from the earliest stages of any project or programme. And the railway must then provide for ongoing risk monitoring and control of the virtual elements of the system, just as is the case for maintaining bits of railway like signals or switches.

For the thousands of different information pathways that a project creates or modifies, each one has to be understood, protected and monitored such that the railway can operate freely under all circumstances.

It isn't an isolated responsibility for a small team of specialists. As railway systems get more and more complex, all practitioners of railway operations and engineering need to understand the implications of virtual and physical security on our infrastructure. At a time of a chronic skills shortage in our industry and across the construction and engineering sector, security is yet another pressure that the railway must endure.

It is also an opportunity. By creating more routes into the industry via these skilled roles, we create the conditions for a wider pool of talent, and potentially one that taps into a younger and more diverse range of people.

On the flip side of this, subterfuge and the reverse-engineering of corporate protectionism may become functions of the industry and necessary subsets of our collective skills if an increasingly profit-driven supply chain has its way.

Back in 2003, Poland's formerly state-owned Nowy Sacz Railway Rolling Stock Repairs Depot in Nowy Sacz, State Independent Enterprise (snappy name) was acquired by a private investor, and a couple of years later changed its name to Newag. It is one of several rail vehicle manufacturers in what is a reasonably buoyant Polish market.

In 2013 it supplied the first of its Impuls electric multiple units to state-owned regional operator Koleje Dolnośląskie (KD), greatly improving the quality of service along their routes. The success of these units led to several further orders. After five years in service, the first trains in the fleet required heavy maintenance, and KD turned to a competitive tender process to identify a supplier. Newag's price was too high, the trains went to Serwis Pojazdów Szynowych (another rail vehicle specialist), and that should have been the end of that.

However, on completion of the necessary overhaul, technicians could not get the trains to restart. Successive attempts, diagnostics and probing could not identify any reason for the trains to have been bricked.

Enter: IT research group Dragon Sector.

Following some Google surfing, KD and their supplier Serwis Pojazdów Szynowych reached out to Dragon Sector researchers, who had previous experience of overcoming corporate self-sabotage, though usually with significantly smaller products.

After weeks of sleuthing, Dragon Sector identified not one, not two, but a succession of deliberate mechanisms coded into the operating system of the trains that would render them inoperable if a series of conditions were met. These conditions included entering the GPS coordinates of Newag's competitor facilities (including one still under construction at the time), replacement of components, remaining static at any location for more than ten days, and even operation past a unit's scheduled maintenance date. These lockout traps were not just found on trains operated by KD, but in Newag trains in use across Poland.

When this story went public in 2023, Newag immediately threatened legal action against both SPS and Dragon Sector, making loud complaints via various official and media channels and claiming insubstantively that its trains had been rendered unsafe to operate. However, in early 2024, their offices were raided by the regional prosecutor's office in Kraków and they rapidly stopped making such a fuss. As I write this, the investigation is still ongoing.

## Crippling private monopolies

Corporate suppliers sabotaging their own products in an attempt to preserve their profit margins is not restricted to software, either. We already discussed some of this in Chapter 2.7, but suffice to say that technological solutions for providing a level interface between trains and platforms exist for all railways, everywhere, but incumbent train manufacturers are unwilling to reshape their designs to accommodate these solutions.

To avoid implementing them, all train manufacturers need to do is ensure that their competitors who do provide level-boarding solutions have saturated order books and then provide such an over-inflated price for their own adaptation of the solution that it is impossible for the operator ordering the train to justify its inclusion, even if that means continuing to exclude passengers from independently travelling by rail.

This is scandalously unacceptable, and is currently the main reason why new trains are still being procured in Britain that do not provide level boarding, despite it now being a proven capability.

What might a solution be? I would suggest that a state-owned rail vehicle manufacturer is one way to overcome this problem; as ever, the "can it go bust?" rule applies. Rail vehicle manufacturers rely on directly or indirectly government-funded contracts to fill their order books, even in Britain with its nominally privatised system. Simultaneously, the collapse of a manufacturer would likely see the state stepping in anyway, at minimum to facilitate transfer of the assets to another company. Given these conditions, it is difficult to argue that these companies exist in any real form of competitive market.

The creation of a state-owned rolling stock manufacturer would not be difficult then, given the (supposed) precipice of precarity that these companies operate on the edge of.

In the recent past, British Rail Engineering Limited (BREL) was the state-owned subsidiary in charge of maintaining and overhauling Britain's existing train fleet and constructing new train fleets. The trains it built were at the cutting edge of rail vehicle technology, most notably the Advanced Passenger Train, the diesel High-Speed Train (the InterCity 125) and two generations of high-speed electric locomotives. BREL also led the design of trains that were then built by other British rolling stock manufacturers, and exported various locomotives, coaches and freight wagons internationally. Many BREL trains are still operating today, not least the Express Sprinters that I grew up with in north east Scotland.

Having already been restructured and part-privatised throughout the 1980s, BREL was sold off via a management buyout in 1989. Amid the drought in new train orders following British Rail's privatisation, sites in Crewe, York and one of the two in Derby were closed. In a classic capitalist monopolisation story, the initial private owners were bought out by Swedish-Swiss conglomerate Asea Brown Boveri, who then merged with Daimler-Benz Transportation, who were then acquired by Bombardier, who then sold the whole lot to Alstom in 2021, resulting in a gigantic monopolistic European train building megacorporation (and one that has received repeated bailouts from the French government). Incidentally, this company also previously bought out the only other major train manufacturer left in Britain in the late twentieth century when it gobbled up Metro-Cammel in Birmingham under its previous guise as GEC Alsthom. It closed this site in 2005.

Meanwhile, in both the UK and USA, what I can only term as "pop-up" factories have replaced long-standing manufacturing sites, appearing at great expense to deliver one or two fleets before either disappearing or winding down production to a drip-feed. This is not a good use of skilled people.

At a time when we need more new rolling stock than at any point in the last hundred years, it is hardly sustainable to rely on an ever-dwindling number of companies, sites and options for building new trains. The fictional notion of a free, private market in train manufacturing needs to be put to bed so that we can concentrate on fulfilling the order book of the future in the most resource-efficient way possible.

This doesn't mean that there is no place for private manufacturers, but given that there is a worldwide shortage in capacity for delivering new rolling stock, it is clear that the "free" market is incapable of meeting the needs of the future, and so the state needs to step in to plug the gap.

This applies not just to trains, but also to the supply of other critical resources and equipment. Signalling equipment is another heavily monopolised domain within the industry, which applies another constraint on the rate at which the railway can upgrade and expand.

Let's deploy the "can it go bust?" rule again: If one of the two major European signalling suppliers fell over, or one of the dominant train manufacturers ceased trading, or (as happened with Carillion) one of the major contractors building and upgrading railways went bust, would these companies be abandoned and left to disappear, taking their capacity (and supply chains) with them? Of course not. Governments would sweep in and either prop them up with accelerated orders or provide them with a bung to keep them afloat.

In which case, the idea that these organisations are actually private is fiction. They are public bodies that pay dividends to shareholders — I don't think I need to expand on the morality or otherwise of this.

As a complex system of systems, the railway requires an enormous range of bits to keep it working, and ensuring a ready, cost-effective supply of these is crucial. Modern supply chains, with their emphasis on just-in-time delivery and minimal warehousing, have been exposed as less than robust by COVID-19, by conflict and by container vessels Austin Powers-ing themselves in the Suez Canal. Any strategic plan must take account of this and consider in-sourcing the supply of these bits where possible.

Lots of the bits will be made by companies that do not fall under the "can it go bust?" rule, and the railway must therefore harness collaboration between private and public entities to deliver them, whether they are trains, under-sleeper pads or lightbulbs, and accordingly must develop the right incentive structure to prevent costs from escalating and private interests from gaining too much power.

## Making change that sticks

The lack of diversity among those people we've charged with planning for our futures contributes greatly to the lack of imagination we see in thinking about that future. Power has been consolidated into a clique of corporate interests, these days no longer just in finance and the old media but across the tech industry as the centre of gravity of non-governmental power has slid in that direction. In the liberal world, the parties both left and right of centre are to a greater or lesser extent in hock to these interests. It isn't conspiratorial to suggest this — power always seeks to consolidate and defend itself. Corporations don't have to be evil to want to protect their perceived short-term interests — by their very nature, private shareholders and those representing them are (little-c) conservative, inflexible and afraid of change for fear of diminishing the size of their pile.

This short-termism, combined with the increasing frenzy of societal challenges and a state with vastly reduced capacity to respond, is compounded by daily news cycles and the rise of political careerism. It has not equipped us with the foresight needed to create meaningful, positive change. Without state capacity, it isn't possible to adequately apply the lessons of the present to the challenges of the future, and consequently even well-meaning efforts in both the public and private sector are often wasted.

Resolving this requires vigorous efforts to reengage society in the functions of democracy. Often, this can be achieved through devolution of power closer to the electorate, empowering local councils and city regions. Citizens assemblies are increasing in popularity, at least as a concept. No matter what the various resolutions might be, the relationship between evidence, accountability and action requires much greater care and thought than is seen today.

But assuming railway systems and the governments that oversee them start enacting the change we've seen, how can we avoid the changes being slowed, halted or reversed?

The first step is through our incentive structure, as we discussed in Chapter 2.2. If we have a legally binding act with cross-party consensus mandating that public transport reach an increased and specific modal share, it becomes very difficult to worm out of making the changes we've talked about without repealing the legislation. Doing this while pretending to deliver emissions reductions would not look convincing to an electorate that, the world over, is polled as caring deeply about global heating and its impacts.

To a great extent, however, responsibility lies with my fellow railway people. We know what railways can deliver, and we need to shout it from the rooftops. No longer can we leave the storytelling to politicians, financiers or techbro sadists — the vision is ours to paint.

And if we are awarded the opportunity to deliver a railway that really kicks the future into top gear, then deliver we must. If people are given a railway system that transforms their lives, they will fight hard not to lose it.

# PART 3

# THE FUTURE

# CHAPTER 3.1

# THINKING BIGGER

A future dominated by sustainable transport is an exciting one. However, the picture painted by futurists rarely describes the best solutions to humankind's mobility problems. Driverless cars, revamped maglev and even flying taxis seem to be the default response when someone asks, "What will the future look like?", yet these transport modes are costly and ineffective.

As with clean water and energy distribution, humans have essentially solved mass transit. There is no more efficient means of carrying things and people across land than a steel wheel on a steel rail. So why aren't the railways inspiring enough to occupy people's vision of the future? Seeing as the challenge is getting those in power to invest, how can this happen if nobody is excited by what railways can achieve?

To inspire people, you need to have a vision. You need to show people how the future could look.

## Sharing the story

The earliest stations were a hotchpotch of styles and forms as the nascent modern railway industry struggled to understand what it was for. As railways began to dominate transport, stations grew into increasingly grand edifices, emanating permanence and telling passengers that the railways were a core part of their lives and the stories of their urban spaces. This tale evolved as railway stations became larger and more overbearing in the early part of the twentieth century.

Following WWII, the story our railways wanted to tell changed for the most part. Stations retreated beneath oversite development. Buildings became more austere. There were some exceptions, as new architectural forms emerged to tell new stories about modernity, cleanliness and speed, but this did not stem the tide, and railway station design withdrew behind the cover of minimum costs and footprints. It's no accident that the relationship between people and their local railways has changed as the station space has evolved.

And this is true of the story the railways tell of themselves and their future. Over their recent history, rail has retreated in the ambition of its view of itself, and this has impacted on how the public perceives it.

There is an interesting paradox that helps us understand why the narrative we weave and not just the raw evidence is critical for building a positive consensus about the way the future should look. Ben Philips, communications director at UNAIDS and author of the book *How to Fight Inequality* calls it the evidence-based paradox. It is instructive.

It is often claimed by campaigners and academics that it's a shortage of evidence that prevents politicians and others from making change happen. However, there is a problem with this. In Ben Phillip's words, "the evidence for transformational change happening because decision-makers are shown evidence is really weak".

Advocates of evidence-based policy by their nature must follow evidence when advocating for the future they want. However, given the evidence confirms that evidence-based policymaking has not consistently and uniformly worked to drive policy change, these advocates must also concede that evidence alone is not enough to shape the future.

If we are to create the future I've talked about giddily throughout this book, then we need to bring the public on board with this — not just politicians, but those who hold them accountable — using passion and imagination as well as evidence. More powerfully still, there is no better way to accelerate change than to have the public pick up and run with these messages, rather than industry and experts alone. If the electorate is shouting about something, change will happen quickly.

Telling the right story, whether through architecture, marketing materials, online services, press releases or social media content, is critical if railways are to be seen as a key part of the future. As we've seen countless times, rail cannot succeed against the onslaught of propaganda from right-wing think-tanks and politicians if it doesn't have the support of the public on its side. On the flip side, get the public on side and positive change is not just probable, it's inevitable.

The story we tell must reach everyone — one size does not fit all. Different communities, age groups and geographies have different needs and therefore need to see different stories reflected back at them. The future I am about to paint cannot be inflicted on society; its development and deployment must be democratically led so that the change it foments can stick. Railways should be exciting. They should be bold. They should be beautiful. But they should also be for everyone.

There is much talk of the need for humanity to broadly and widely minimise travel, hunker down and hide to minimise our carbon emissions and weather the worst impacts of climate change. This is wrong on two fronts.

Firstly, slowing, stopping or reversing the amount we travel will not change the behaviour of the wealthiest in society, who will always find a way to justify their own mobility. What travelling less to save the planet materially means, therefore, is retaining the status quo of who gets to travel.

This is not to say that there isn't an enormous amount of superfluous travel engaged in by the rich and powerful that can be reduced and indeed in many cases eradicated. The unregulated rise of private jet flights has been hugely damaging to the planet while offering no benefit to society whatsoever. But suggesting that it is all of us, as individuals, that need to travel less to save the planet shifts the blame away from the guilty. As we have explored already, across the globe people have been locked into polluting and personally expensive car dependency by decades of pro-car policy. Aviation has dominated where rail could have provided better alternatives. These were systematic choices led by a coalition of governments and corporate interests, and it is not our personal responsibility to correct these choices; it is a collective one.

The dominance of car-oriented development is chronic across most of the planet. Railways are a key component in reversing this trend, and understanding what this looks like can also offer a chance to reevaluate how we shape human spaces, helping us to thrive as individuals and communities.

The second reason why minimising travel to save the planet is wrong is one that is deeply important to me: it is painfully, aggressively unimaginative.

Humanity has an innate desire to explore, to enlarge our horizons and to learn. The more of society that has access to travel, either through better transport enabling easier travel or better working conditions allowing them freedom to travel, the closer together we feel as a society. The kinship we feel with our siblings around the planet emboldens *and educates* us to tackle society's injustices. Travel should not be restricted to the entitled rich or to middle-class NGO volunteers; the more time we spend learning about other people, other cultures and other struggles, the more we can learn to tackle our own challenges.

Diverse teams are better at solving problems, and what better way to widen the pool of that diversity than through better global transport systems, sharing our knowledge internationally and outside of the potentially narrow views of the global north?

We have the technology to make this sort of connectivity a reality. Over distances greater than 1,000 km, rail will never be faster than flying, though greatly improved rail can make international rail travel across continents more realistic. While emissions-free aviation is at best unlikely this century, it is possible for rail to tackle such a high percentage of short- and medium-distance flights that there can be room within humanity's carbon budget to allow for long-distance flights to keep operating.

Nobody advocating for a clean, healthy and equitable future for society should be afraid of building for speed. Perhaps counterintuitively, the faster a railway system, the cheaper it is to operate. High speeds mean you need fewer trains, which means smaller train maintenance facilities depots. Faster throughput means you can get away with smaller stations, which means less environmental impact, particularly in densely built-up city centres where disruption is extensive and land is expensive.

Indeed, successive studies have determined that high-speed rail is the only mode of transport that is cost positive when accounting for all externalities — that is, all of the up-front and hidden costs associated with a given mode of transport.

But we're getting ahead of ourselves. Earlier in the book, I talked about the need to think about the challenges humanity is facing in terms of the timescales over which we are acting. Accordingly, it makes sense to think about how railways can respond to these challenges now, within the next decade, by the middle of this century, and by the end of the century. It may seem abstract to thank that far into the future, but given we design and build railways today to be operating in the mid-2100s, I don't think it's so ridiculous.

## To 2030: getting our ducks in a row

The first and most important step in delivering the railways of the future is to set the aspirational modal shift targets, bound into law, that will steer the shape of transport up to and beyond 2050.

These must be supported by a wider policy framework — railways do not exist in a vacuum. Road pricing and other forms of usage-based charging would better represent the cost of driving for users, and would distribute costs towards those who choose to drive rather than those who have to. Market-warping policies such as low taxes on aviation fuel, tax relief for new cars, and free or subsidised parking will have been consigned to history, helping to reverse a century of artificially sustained private transport growth.

Collaboration must be accelerated to promote the sharing of best practice in technical and operational standards, ensuring that rail is as cheap as possible to operate and expand worldwide. Railways and public transport providers are not and should not be competing with each other — they are competing with private transport (and potentially the bullshit transport systems that the tech industry is desperate to foist on us).

With the modal shift mission set, countries must devolve and distribute power over railways to where it is most effectively harnessed. People need to feel like they have ownership over their transport systems to use them, and the development, specification and funding of transport projects, as well as the way in which the resulting networks are run, should match the scale of those networks. To achieve this will require many more practitioners in planning and other back-room disciplines than we have today, and a return of that experience from the private to the public sector.

Indeed, building state capacity is a key component in solving an enormous number of problems, particularly in the UK. Britain's planning woes can mostly be traced to the evisceration of council budgets and headcounts since the 1990s (and before), with constant austerity policies and centralisation wiping out planning teams with local passion and knowledge. As power is devolved to local, regional and city authorities, they need to grow their capacity to plan. Get this right, and not only can you develop strategic plans that deliver on modal shift targets at all levels of government, but you can also review those plans as time passes, shaping and reshaping them to reflect success and failure. In turn, this can feed into appraisal at a project level, too.

You don't measure the need to build a bridge by counting the number of people who swim across a river, and yet this is very much the basis for determining demand for future rail projects in today's world. Appraisal has its place when considering options or the prioritisation of projects. However, and for the most part, transport appraisal is usually used to confirm decisions already made for political reasons, and consequently such analysis instead provides a nice, lucrative feedback loop for consultants, allowing the wasting of millions today to avoid investing billions for the future. If there is a political desire for a region to have a railway connection, then the first question should not be whether it will be worth it, but rather how do we best deliver it, and this attitude should permeate decision-making.

For many authorities, transport appraisal guidelines have been improved in recent years and now do a better job of accounting for the benefits of linking deprived areas rather than focusing purely on areas that will generate maximum revenue. This will be key in prioritising the delivery of any nation's strategic plan. Areas with low-earning populations will also usually be areas with reduced car ownership, so improved public transport is a lifeline.

Deprivation is one metric, but plenty of others exist. The area of transport economics is heavily under-developed when compared to, say, health economics, and there is a significant opportunity for academic work to better understand the relationships between transport outputs and transport outcomes.

Appraisal is only one part of the picture, though. For the railway system to truly deliver for the populations served by it and funding it, they need to have a greater input into the shape of its development.

However, as the strategic plans develop, the way these plans are consulted upon is crucial — such consultations cannot be tick-box exercises, not least as involving local populations can lead to greatly improved outcomes and much quicker delivery, as local buy-in can overcome the hurdles of the planning process.

Of course, there is a need to resist certain pressures from campaigners who may be very excited about their local project but who do not have the broader view — or whose view of the future is skewed by nostalgia. In countries where well-developed railway networks were contracted in the twentieth century, it's important to remember that, just because closing a railway was a bad idea doesn't mean reopening it is a good idea. Indeed, the idea of railway reopenings should be treated with extreme caution. Lost railways were built for the past, and rarely serve today's geography optimally. Only new railways should be built, even if these make use of some or most of a former trackbed.

Mitigating habitat loss is also crucial, and I've already spoken about how rail's greater capacity for movement can limit sprawl and overall transport land-use, thus protecting our precious landscapes and biospheres. The arguments of those who are unconvinced of these merits should not be dismissed out of hand, and planners and designers should not be complacent. Railways which truly serve the people must sustain the ecosystems we rely on for survival, but this should be seen in context. Rail's impact on habitat is tiny compared to that of road projects being built across the world today. Car dependence is driving more and more local road building and other highway-based urban sprawl such as out-of-town commercial and industrial developments. This is a case that we need to make clearly and patiently, armed with both evidence and passion for the right future.

In all, this will require better communication of ideas and evidence to the public and the politicians representing them. Engineers have to be good communicators, certainly, but they're also busy actually designing and building the railways, so we need many more dedicated communicators who understand the nuts and bolts and the needs of the people we are trying to deliver for.

As national and regional plans are published, and as delivery of these plans picks up pace, the workforce of the railway across all domains will necessarily expand. As this happens, it is critical that great care is taken at all levels to grow the diversity of teams, to celebrate that diversity and to embed it by providing working conditions that do not exclude people based on their circumstances. In this, unions have a key role to play.

As for costs, new or upgraded railways may require significant upfront investment, but these costs are more than covered by the benefits to society of taking cars and HGVs off the roads. For comparison, the total annual expenditure of the UK railway is around £20bn. The total annual expenditure on roads is around £46bn. Much of the railway costs are fixed, and increased usage of the existing network would result in limited additional costs, whereas increased road usage will result in significant additional costs, primarily resulting from the increased fatalities and serious injuries resulting from road collisions.

Meanwhile, road's costs (and rail's benefits) omit externalities such as health costs from pollution and physical inactivity, the ecological costs of roads and the ultimate cost of climate change. What's more, roads demand an enormous volume of land-take owing to their relatively low capacity. A two-track railway can carry ten or twenty times more people per hour than a six-lane motorway can.

I've spent some of the book being a bit mean about buses, but I shall take this chance to say that buses are the allies of the railway. Without good bus networks, rail simply cannot achieve its required modal shift targets. Buses must feed railways where population densities are not well suited to rail. They can parallel metro or rural rail systems to feed intermediate stops between railway stations. They can be responsive to change, and can build public transport usage in readiness for more permanent solutions. And good bus networks are impossible in unregulated conditions such as those in the UK outside of London. Buses need to be integrated into railway timetables, they need to be frequent, and they need to fall under the same devolved control as railways do.

## To 2040: building for change

By 2030, countries with currently dysfunctional railway organisations need to have implemented new structures and have evaluated and tweaked them as required as strategic plans move into the delivery phase. They need to have developed and be starting the delivery of their strategic plans, having passed the legislation to bind into law the necessary modal shift targets to meet net zero.

Doing so will create the space and the lines of communication to foster far greater and more useful innovation in the transport sector than happens now, with the speed of development and deployment concurrently increasing. In turn, these can be incorporated into projects and wider strategic plans as they are revisited, reviewed, evaluated and developed.

We've talked a lot, too much probably, about passenger rail (sincere apologies, logistics wonks), but what will the freight sector have done by this point to deliver a sustainable future? We know that road haulage has a disproportionately negative impact on highway maintenance budgets, on air quality (particularly in cities) and on road safety. The haulage industry is also suffering from a chronic shortage of drivers. Even if there are successful mass deployments of electric haulage vehicles, these will be immensely heavy and will damage roads and facilities if relied upon in equivalent numbers to today. So by 2030, rail will have had to take a greater share.

At the same time, the introduction of reduced- or zero-emission zones in our cities, as well as the necessary pursuit of zero-fatality cities, will eliminate the last-mile advantages of moving goods by road. As soon as there is a need for trans-shipment from trucks to vans or cargo bikes at the fringes of the urban core, road loses its advantage over rail. At this point, the greater efficiency of rail haulage will drive a significant modal shift of freight away from roads, even under existing regulatory and market conditions. By next decade, rail must be ready for this change.

One of the key challenges for the condensing and municipalisation of urban logistics and for better bus provision is that publicly owned city centre industrial space (such as former postal facilities or bus depots) has been divested over successive decades. To provide sufficient capacity for the level of goods delivery we see today, and indeed to augment integrated transport services with increased bus frequencies, more space is needed for transshipment from larger vehicles to smaller ones.

Thinking strategically, a suitably capable, devolved authority could exploit this as an opportunity to reverse the loss of this logistics space while also decreasing private motor vehicle capacity. One thing that few cities across the world are truly short of is car parking. In the UK, much of the land occupied by car parks in city centres is adjacent to or at least close to existing or former railways. You can fill in the metaphorical (and physical) gaps.

Meanwhile, railways should not be afraid to own and harness open or developed spaces adjacent to (or under) their lines in the urban and rural realm. In many countries, the railways are some of if not the largest single landowners. The chance to exploit this position — one that will only be cemented by further railway expansion — to create public spaces for culture, recreation, independent businesses and community groups is enormous and cannot be missed.

In the UK, by 2030 even a contract-expiry approach to ending privatisation ought to have concluded, and city regions should have been handed the level of control over their own rail systems that they feel matches their needs.

The railways in all of those "delivering" countries in the Top Twenty we established in Chapter 1.3 share many of the same deep-rooted challenges. However, those countries on the European mainland have seen much greater levels of cumulative (if not recent) investment in some high-speed rail infrastructure and, more importantly, at a city-region level in many excellent urban and suburban railway systems, including trams and metros. Meanwhile, the UK has seen vanishingly little investment in urban rail capacity outside of London, and has been in an organisational crisis with a vacuum of leadership since the May 2018 timetable collapse. By the 2030s, this needs to have been reversed.

While casting meaningful nets around city regions is a complex and contentious issue, taking urban area populations as defined by the Office of National Statistics gives six cities in the UK with a population greater than one million people. Those are London, Manchester, Birmingham, Leeds, Glasgow and Liverpool (and their surrounding regions). Of these, only two have metro systems (one of which is the diminutive Glasgow Subway, which, though I'm very fond of it, barely counts). Four of them have reasonably well-segregated suburban rail systems. Three have trams.

Looking to the UK's close neighbours on the continent, it is common to see cities with over a million people having multi-line metro systems bolstered by suburban rail. Trams are commonplace in cities of over half a million people, of which there are fourteen in the UK (and only four with trams).

By 2040 we must have broken down the legal, regulatory and funding barriers that prevent the right type of transport technology being applied to the desired level of demand. It is not right that cities have to deploy buses where trams would be more appropriate for the level of demand, or that they have to rely on trams ("light rail" doesn't exist, it's a political euphemism) where a full-blown metro is needed to satisfy the public need for mobility. The technology must meet the desired capacity as determined by future modal shift, not merely incremental growth.

We've already established that Austria and Switzerland operate two of the best railway systems in the world, resulting in a high modal share. However, driving further improvements will require further capacity, and squeezing more out of their existing network is going to become increasingly challenging over the next decade. Both countries need to plan now for additional capacity via the addition of new lines — ideally high-speed lines — not just for providing increased capacity headroom for domestic services, but also to unlock wider European modal shift. Both countries sit on the paths between Northern and Southern Europe, and between Eastern and Western Europe, and so most long journeys across the continent intersect with their networks in some way. Domestic journeys may not be hugely impacted by the lack of high-speed services thanks to shorter distances and high frequencies, but journeys crossing through these countries would be greatly assisted by the creation of new high-speed lines paralleling the trunk routes. Work to plan these should start now, and construction could commence by the end of the 2020s.

China and India have different challenges, both to the other two "elite" national systems and to each other. China has well-developed networks of high-speed, freight and urban rail, and other than duplication, there's little that network expansion can now achieve to drive modal shift. China relies on significant road usage, particularly in terms of freight haulage, and so policies to reduce road usage are critical in driving modal share, perhaps more so than rail-focused policies. Conversely, India has a high-speed rail network to build, and is already getting on with it. If its pace of electrification has been anything to go by, it will have largely finished this high-speed network by 2040.

Such major civil engineering work has a carbon cost — the construction of new high-speed railways can emit tens of millions of tonnes of CO2 equivalent. However, this should be compared with (for example) the shift to private electric cars, which for the UK alone will emit 400–600 million tonnes of CO2 equivalent just for a single like-for-like replacement (to say nothing of the rapid rate at which the automotive industry encourages people to buy new cars).

To be attractive to many users, the railway must get closer to their homes, businesses and leisure destinations. New stations and lines in both urban and rural areas are required to take more people off the road network. And particularly in rural areas, the speed that trains travel at should be increased. Upgrades to track and signalling, including straightening out alignments where necessary, will further encourage people out of their cars. Across railway networks, the control systems that manage signalling, traffic and communications must continue to be upgraded and automated, reducing maintenance costs, increasing safety and minimising disruption to the railway by moving equipment away from the track and into trains.

As new capacity is created and in turn soaked up by modal shift and the trains needed to fulfil it, pressure on the railway operations and the sharing of track access will mount, as it already has in the UK today. Among other important considerations regarding the balance between different domestic operators, this will require an evaluation of the role of open-access operators. These organisations have been said to create competition and improve services, which may be true on lines where excess capacity exists. But as we sweat our assets to maximise modal shift while minimising resource exploitation, this capacity will thin, and the essentially extractive nature of open-access operations will be exposed. These services would not exist without the investments made by incumbent railway organisations into, for example, skills and facilities.

Ultimately, competition should not be between railway operators but with road and air. This similarly applies to the leasing of train fleets. This model may work in some conditions, such as for a city or regional operator leasing trains from the national railway organisation, but the existence of dedicated rolling stock leasing companies is a bottleneck on the delivery of new trains and represents one of the largest leaks of subsidies into private hands in the railway industry.

As this decade ends, railways will become high-skill, high-employment systems that can provide new roles and opportunities for people displaced from other sectors. They can be a model for understanding the useful application of automation to make better use of a growing workforce, not a justification for diminishing it.

By 2040, we need to have loosened the grip of car dominance on our society. In turn, this will greatly alter our approach to spatial planning for people, business and industry. I've laid out some of the ways we can achieve this here, but clearly a polemic non-fiction book from an upstart railway engineer can only cover so much. However, if we get this right, it points us all in the same direction to start really building momentum in how we maximise and grow our mobility sustainably.

## To 2050: reaping the rewards

As we move beyond this horizon towards 2050, harnessing national and international cooperation to develop transport plans across modes can unleash rail's potential to maximise the benefits of urban living. Such plans may look to the middle of the century; others may look further into the future still.

Let's take some examples of key corridors of human habitation that haven't yet been united by effective rail links and ought to be by the middle of the century: China has linked almost all of its dense corridors, mainland Europe is getting there, and India has its own plans for high-speed expansion. The 800-km, near straight line between Quebec City and Toronto is home to 50% of the Canadian population. It currently takes over twelve hours to cover the distance by public transport, yet a conventional high-speed line could enabled the distance to be covered in three. This would obliterate the journey-time benefits that currently exist for those who drive it in seven hours, and by the time you've accounted for reaching and then hanging about in airports, three hours would be competitive with flights as well.

A further 800 km of straight line would connect these cities to Detroit and Chicago, enabling 6.5-hour transit times from Chicago to Quebec, linking forty million people to each other, nearly the population of the Northeast Corridor. Combine hub stations at each of the major cities with robust regional and commuter rail systems, and overlay tram and metro systems in the dense urban cores, and you would take an enormous bite out of the modal share of both road and air.

Capturing the same number of people but along a much shorter and more densely populated corridor, a high-density, mixed-use line along the West African coast could link Ghana's capital of Accra with Lagos, Nigeria's largest city, in around four hours versus the current ten hours it takes to drive. The 400-km corridor would include Togo's capital of Lomé and Benin's capital Porto-Novo. It would unify the legacy mixed-gauge railways that stretch inland — they were built by the colonial powers to extract mineral and resource wealth from each of these countries and consequently do not provide a network suitable for the modern needs of the region. Such a line would also supercharge the patchy aspirations of the Economic Community of West African States to expand the standard-gauge rail network of its member states to enable free movement of people and goods and to maximise tourism. The existing highway connection along this coast linking the four countries is already severely congested, particularly in and around the major cities, and an environmentally and economically sustainable alternative will be necessary this half of the century.

Having been in planning for two decades in some form, the 500-km corridor linking Campinas, São Paulo and Rio de Janeiro would bring together a population of fifty million people and provide journey times of less than three hours between the three cities. This is one of the most populated regions on earth.

If we want to get really geopolitically spicy, then another high-speed corridor would be from Egypt's capital in Cairo up to Port Said and along the Mediterranean coast linking through Palestine, Israel, Jordan, Lebanon, Syria and into Turkey. It would be a 1,000 km railway, and could link Cairo to Gaziantep in five hours. This corridor includes some of the world's most densely populated urban areas, including those in Palestine. Such a line is currently a political fantasy (other than in the mind of US president Joe Biden, who talked about it in a rather rambling speech on Israel delivered in 2023), but until this corridor is served by rail, there is no sustainable means by which to travel between these cities. Any list of unserved, dense population corridors that omits it is incomplete. Work to develop these lines could start now, but the political (as much if not more than the engineering) complexity would make these slow projects to deliver. But deliver them we must: such densely populated corridors of humanity cannot survive the future without a sustainable transport spine linking them together.

Meanwhile, before 2050 Europe needs to have completed its high-speed rail network. This includes the UK, which by this point will need lines linking beyond the great northern cities of Leeds and Manchester into the North East and Scotland. Elsewhere, missing links that can bring the edges of Europe within a day's travel of its core should be operating with decent frequencies. Such lines would allow journeys from Paris to Istanbul in fifteen hours — so a long day, but a day nonetheless.

North America, too, needs to have had a transport revolution to match the construction of the US interstate system. All of the major cities of the continent, including across the US and Mexican border, should be connected by rail, and measures to limit the dominance of aviation needs to match this level of ambition.

The same must be true for the Indian subcontinent and southeast Asia, given the scale of population across this huge sweep of the planet. And in all of the million-plus cities in the world, of which there may be as many as eight hundred by 2050, segregated high-quality metro networks will be required to move populations around safely, comfortably and efficiently. Metros, by the way, require the following: dedicated tracks, no on-street running, steel wheels on steel rails and system capacities of 20,000 or more. No other application of railway or transport technology is able to shift the same volumes of people to keep these cities mobile.

In the last quarter century, the average land consumed by urban residents has increased in 60% of the world's cities. Rail can and must reverse this trend. Smaller cities will have lighter (in terms of system capacity) metros, suburban rail and trams. In all cases, the proliferation of better public transport will not just follow a city's organic development but will lead it. The agglomeration effects of improved public transport can be compounded by transport-led development, unlocking better choices and opportunities for its residents. Usefully for our environment and carbon emissions in particular, the world is urbanising, and public transport is how we deliver the homes, jobs, services and playtime that these populations need.

By this point, climate change–instigated drought will have rendered the Panama Canal inoperable for much of the year, and rail will be the only viable alternative. As with municipal logistics, this may shift the balance away from shipping entirely for some international flows of goods, though it is worth highlighting that the environmental and social impacts of "conquering" the Darién Gap between the continents of North and South America are unconscionable — it is one flow where rail does not have a place.

The same will be true for the Suez Canal, though its consistent elevation means it isn't the availability of water that will limit its use. Instead, increased heat will result in more dust and sandstorms sweeping across from the Sinai and Sahara deserts, reducing ships' ability to operate and potentially burying the canal if dredging becomes too expensive. Here, however, rail can provide an alternative, allowing a complete bypass of the Mediterranean Sea for flows between Europe and Asia. The scale of change to global supply chains this will result in cannot be overstated, but the end of uninterrupted use of these two critical logistical pinch points is a certainty.

Finally, a key response by the arbiters of the international railway network must be to actually create an international railway network. Standardisation of track gauge was first sought in the 1840s, but we've yet to achieve it. To enable global supply chains to rely first and foremost on rail, we need to remove the physical barriers breaking the flow of mobility between the global regions. As the biggest culprit of this, Russia and its former imperial or Soviet constituent states need to correct their rail networks to standard gauge. Spain and Portugal — you're on the list too. In your own time, of course.

## To 2100: a new world

Reach beyond 2050 to the end of the century and this is where we get to dream big. By this point, we'll be witnessing great changes in our built environment. Once seen as vital in keeping economies moving, the wide strips of concrete and tarmac highways snaking across our urban realm will now be seen as shackles holding our cities back. We'll be digging them up or bringing them down, using the freed space to create linear parks, new communities or new lines of suburban rail transport.

Though the effects of climate change cannot be fully mitigated, significantly better transport networks will have reshaped patterns of land use and resource extraction to minimise the impact on biodiversity and the natural environment, with impacts falling far more fairly — no longer will the places seeing the greatest impact be the ones least responsible for the causes.

Across the globe, huge swathes of land, sometimes as large as the cities they serviced, were once given over to airports and the industries they sustain. Thanks to high-speed rail links between cities and nations wiping out aviation's market share, many of these will have been replaced by new mixed-use districts, swapping aviation for innovation in green technologies such as energy generation or train assembly.

Instead, huge flows of people across long distances will be facilitated by excellent international links. These ribbons of opportunity won't just be used by people travelling to attend university, visit family or seek adventure, but will be a lifeline for those fleeing the increasingly capricious climate and its consequences. They will act as the blood vessels facilitating the seasonal pulse of food production around the planet to ensure equal worldwide distribution, and will be able to respond quickly to climate-induced famines, crop failures or other calamities.

Current flows of migrants will have been radically redrawn as climate change pushes weather extremes beyond the extent to which countries can cope. Bangladesh is an example of a country uniquely vulnerable to the effects of rising sea levels and more violent storms, with one in seven of its inhabitants likely to have been displaced by semi-permanent flooding by the middle of this century. Given its current — and rapidly rising — population, perhaps as many as twenty-five million people will be pushed from their homes. Incidentally, Bangladesh already houses the world's largest refugee population thanks to the ongoing genocide of Rohingya people in western Myanmar.

As historian Patrick Wyman puts it, "Mobility is the single greatest human asset for dealing with adverse climatic conditions." Globalisation offers opportunities if its processes and tools are harnessed by everyone, rather than by those few who benefit from the current exploitation of cheap labour and sparse regulation. With links across the planet so greatly improved, there will no longer be the ability to exploit pockets of workers, and so rather than replacing humans, automation will ensure that the productivity of a well-paid workforce is maintained and that a more skilled workforce spends as little time in manual labour as possible.

Battery electric vehicles may be the future of cars, but they are certainly not the future of transport. The proliferation of walkable cities, facilitated by the ineffectiveness of the car compared to rail-based alternatives, means that vulnerable people will be less reliant on social services to live independent lives, allowing those resources to be focused on those still in need. Disabled people will no longer be trapped by inaccessible public transport or reliant on driving or being driven. They will have access to the same opportunities as everyone else using public transport.

The freedom afforded to everyone, including vulnerable or young people, can greatly improve our collective wellbeing and mental health. Loneliness will decline, and health will improve as air quality does. People will be more active as the number of people having to own a car plummets. Reflected by the change in the way we move about, the shift of society away from individualism towards a more collective view will help us surpass our differences and lose interest in populism.

The ability of our democratic structures to deliver a future where railways are the circulatory system of our civilisation will be an almighty test of political functionality. But just as taking your blood pressure gives a good picture of your health, the constant evaluation of the effectiveness of railway systems can provide a guide to the health of a democracy, and can allow for corrective measures to be prescribed.

Because we cannot fumble this bag. We owe it to the next generation and the one after that to hand them a planet that we've at least attempted to fix after the generations before us screwed it up. Now is the time to go big, face up to the challenge ahead of us and get on with tackling it.

2100 is not so far off. My daughter will only be 77. This future is not just possible; it's necessary, and it's within reach.

We know why we are building rail into the fabric of our future, but we need to apply equal care as to *how* we do this — because the legacy we leave will be a permanent one. The story we tell about the railways — and the story we design the railways themselves to tell — will be crucial in ensuring their development harnesses the best rather than the worst of humanity's tendencies.

If we don't get that story right, as we've seen countless times as major railway projects have stalled or been abandoned, then we cannot unlock the sustainable future that they necessarily must be a part of. If we do get it right, the opportunities are boundless, and the message should reflect this in its scale and optimism.

Once a weapon of oppression, railways can and should be a tool for hope.

# CODA

# WHAT'S NEXT?

Mobility is inherently a shared endeavour, by choice or not. Building systems of mobility that embrace this, giving people their time and space back in the process, can help us build a more collectively minded society that believes more strongly in shared endeavour and our shared struggle. And doing this with flare can bring us more than shared utility: travel can and should be joyous, and joy is multiplied when it is shared.

For many people, mobility is wrapped up in their working lives, and so by making rail travel the default choice, and by making it as fast and fluid as possible, we can give them their time back. We can decouple working from thriving, giving us all more time to see friends and family, enjoy culture, wild spaces, sport — in other words, time to explore what it means to be alive.

Given what railways can do, they are the key to unlocking this shared future. We will work together to build this future, and we will reap its rewards together, too.

## A better world

This boom in the size and importance of railways cannot be allowed to return them to being a tool for imperialism and mass exploitation. To avoid this happening, we need a mass shift in the centre of power away from existing elites and towards the rest of society. We need a rebalancing of diplomatic power away from incumbent economic powers and towards those countries on whom we rely for our resources, those countries who have been historically exploited and those currently facing the onslaught of global heating's ravages.

A tool in the wrong hands can become a weapon.

Isolationism, nationalism, the othering of minority populations — the ratcheting up of this rhetoric by leaders desperate to perpetuate their grip on power leads to war. As I write this, there are five major global conflicts killing tens of thousands of people a year: the Myanmar civil war, the renewed civil war in Sudan, the three-way conflict in Azawad in northern Mali, Russia's invasion of Ukraine and the genocide being inflicted by Israel on Palestine.

I'm not so naïve to think that humankind's propensity for war will evaporate if we better connect our regions and encourage the erosion of isolationism in the process. Climate change is being exacerbated by war, just as war will increasingly be waged over the challenges that climate change creates, such as access to resources, diminished availability of land, and mass migration to escape extreme weather — all on a scale not yet conceived of.

Indeed, railways have been visible in recent years, not as instruments of peace, but as part of the machine of war or territorial aggression. Russia's use of railways for military logistics in Ukraine and the construction of the Kerch Strait Bridge to provide a fixed link to the Crimean peninsula stand as examples of railways used for aggression, even if these have been countered to an extent by Ukraine's feats of engineering and operational heroics in keeping its railways running during the ongoing war, often under Russian bombardment.

The Chenab Railway Bridge in Kashmir is the highest in the world and sits on a railway line that is certainly an engineering marvel, with its full opening imminent. However, this line has been built partly to enable the dilution of Indian Kashmir's largely Muslim population as part of the wider ethnonationalist project of India's current government. China has also used railway construction to homogenise populations in its more ethnically diverse outer provinces.

Nevertheless, railways can be deployed as tools of diplomacy to forge stronger ties that diminish the chance of future conflict. India is also collaborating with its bordering neighbours — even Pakistan — to improve rail links across the subcontinent. As a counterbalance to China's imperial manoeuvres, Indonesia has been exporting railway expertise to countries across Southeast Asia, building diplomatic ties in the process. Turkey and its neighbours in the eastern Mediterranean and Persian Gulf have been centring diplomatic efforts on the former Hejaz Railway and a possible extension into Istanbul as originally envisaged by the Ottomans. Even closer to reality is the Gulf Cooperation Council's Gulf Railway network linking the Persian Gulf states, with aspirations for links via Saudi Arabia's own proposed rail system northwards towards Turkey. These latter two examples are as much petro-dollar vanity as tangible projects, but their construction would still represent meaningful and valuable ties, particularly if the lines reached countries on the Mediterranean Sea.

Most recently, the All-Island Rail Review in Ireland has enabled the authorities on both sides of Western Europe's most hotly contested border to build stronger working relationships to deliver what will eventually be much stronger physical ties.

Only the railway is capable of moving large numbers of people or goods quickly and safely. Call me a fantasist, but coupling stronger international bonds forged in cooperation and friendship with a greatly expanded and improved international railway network may provide humanity with its greatest tool to respond to the growing nature of climate change's threats. Taking food and water into areas of famine, or evacuating people from areas threatened by flooding or other extreme weather calamities may be the only way to keep our population safe over the next century. We've seen railways used this way recently — barely hours after Russia began its invasion of mainland Ukraine, evacuation trains began taking what would end up being nearly four million people to safety away from the frontline or into neighbouring countries on its western border.

Ultimately, global cooperation is a necessary precursor to resolving many of the biggest challenges we've explored, which in turn will enable national and local governments to focus on the challenges they are better equipped to tackle. But building the trust needed for this cooperation is hugely challenging. Progress has been made in creating agreement at an international level, at least in terms of the scale of some of the problems, but coordinating meaningful global action on (for example) climate change has proven almost impossible up to this point.

More than any other shared diplomatic endeavour, the collaboration of countries to create the new corridors of mobility I described in Part 3 would be hugely productive and positive. Such projects, enormous and internationally involved as they would necessarily be, offer the chance to be the great unifiers of regions previously riven with mistrust and prejudice.

Railways created the modern world, with all its ills, and enabled capitalism to overtake mercantilism as the world's dominant economic dogma. What better way to move us into the future than securing railways from capital and harnessing them for social good? For me at least, it would be the ultimate signifier of a shift into a much more positive future, and a satisfying gob of spit in the eye of private capital and its desperate need to destroy everything on the pyre of wealth accumulation.

We can do this together, and the railways are how we get there.

# AFTERWORD

I hope that I've made the case for railways not just as a crucial component in keeping our species mobile, but as a tool for repairing many other aspects of our society that we've managed to break in our unerring race for power and wealth.

There are surely many more stories to tell and much more data out there to help fill in the gaps — I've only really scratched the surface with this book. Part of the reason I was delighted to be asked to write this book by Repeater is that it gave me the chance to think about and pull together lots of disparate ides into the one narrative. In doing so, I also hope I've sparked some thoughts in the minds of others, no matter what their domain.

Academics, in particular, reach out: I want to hear your stories and explore your work to see how it reinforces, or perhaps undermines, the picture I've painted. I think there's more to say about the movement of goods and how it can be integrated with a shift in our society away from consumerism. I've danced around the subject of costs, both when it comes to building and operating railways (mostly because I think these costs should follow, not lead, the specification of the railway system we want to have) and with regard to the fares and rates facing passengers and freight customers wanting to use them.

I also don't think I've done justice to the global picture, not least away from Europe and the anglosphere, and I would love to explore how my incentive frameworks can be applied to communities the world over.

Now, a few thanks — firstly to Tariq and Repeater for taking a punt on a political railway book written by an eager but chaotic-minded engineer. Josh and Chris: your support and accommodation of my hopeless relationship with deadlines meant this thing could come into existence in parallel with a vibrant, beautiful baby whose relationship with sleep is almost as dreadful. Both of you have steered and moulded what was a big pile of words into something I'm truly proud of. Thanks to those across the rail industry who have stuck their neck out for me over the years — including those of you in the Young Rail Professionals, in my professional institution and in my union (the rightly proud RMT). Thanks to the supporters of #Railnatter, my little podcast that has somehow ballooned beyond what I could ever have expected — as this goes to publication, it isn't far off one million views/listens. Thanks to the Kitchen in Osbaldwick, where I wrote a decent chunk of the book; the repetitive suburbs of the UK desperately lack the community heart that you bring to our corner of York. More than a little thanks goes to my friends and co-conspirators for the patience you've had with my lack of responsiveness over the last year or so. The greatest thanks, though, must go to my wonderful wife. Dina, you are my everything, and without your support it isn't just that this book wouldn't exist, I'd be immeasurably diminished without the energy, knowledge and perspective you've given me each day of the last ten years.

The final thing I want to address is what you, the reader, can do to make what I've written about a reality. If you're a journalist, I've hopefully helped you to frame your stories slightly differently, and provided you the tools to cut through some of the bullshit that gets thrown your way by the dominant tech, automotive and aviation industries of today. Politicians: you've an opportunity to harness railways as part of your story while leaving a legacy you can be proud of. Activists, aficionados, campaigners, environmentalists and social scientists: we have a duty to work together to make change happen and to create the stories that fuel the change. Let's listen to each other — we know that evidence alone is not enough to create good policy: it takes fury; it takes passion and it takes grit. We can all provide this in our own way, big or small.

Right back at the start I described the tome you're holding as a handbook, and handbooks are supposed to deliver instructions. So here's my instruction: take the train. And if you can't take the train, bother someone who has the power to change that.

# REPEATER BOOKS

is dedicated to the creation of a new reality. The landscape of twenty-first-century arts and letters is faded and inert, riven by fashionable cynicism, egotistical self-reference and a nostalgia for the recent past. Repeater intends to add its voice to those movements that wish to enter history and assert control over its currents, gathering together scattered and isolated voices with those who have already called for an escape from Capitalist Realism. Our desire is to publish in every sphere and genre, combining vigorous dissent and a pragmatic willingness to succeed where messianic abstraction and quiescent co-option have stalled: abstention is not an option: we are alive and we don't agree.